3/15/14

Enjoy these
Memories

Sarah Senkbeil

Company's Coming

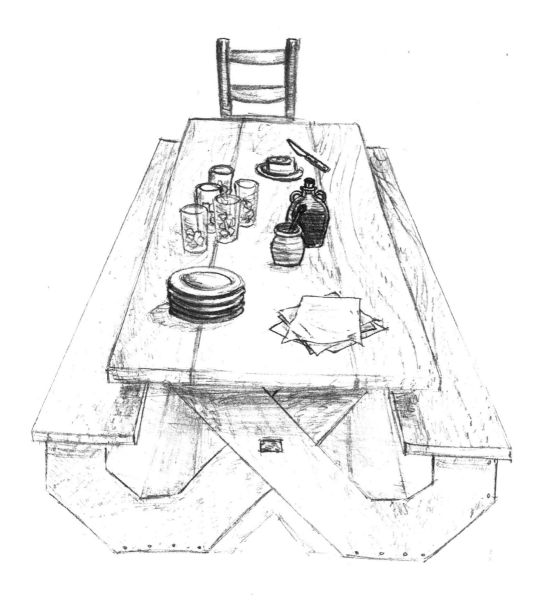

By: Sarah Senkbeil

ISBN # 978-1-935802-05-1

**FATHER
&
SON**
PUBLISHING, INC.
4909 North Monroe Street
Tallahassee, Florida 32303-7015
www.fatherson.com
800-741-2712

Preface

As the author of "Company's Coming," I have so many people who have encouraged me to keep on writing. They insist they want copies of this as I have been writing about times they remember. They can relate to them.

Myra Stephens loaned me a tobacco stick to be able to measure and describe.

I had typed my book on a typewriter and was told that it had to be on computer or else it would not be publishable. I had used whatever typewriter was available at the time, so it was done on several different typewriters.

Never having used a computer before, I went to the library. The workers there were so gracious to me and helped me so much; Vickie Young and Kathy Varnadoe especially. When calling on someone to help me, they were there. I hand -typed several thousand words on the computer and then hit the wrong key and erased it all. I had to start again. Then my husband became ill and passed away.

I met a young man, Joshua Cooper, at the library and asked him to copy the work from my typewriting on his home computer. But, he soon became too busy and returned the material.

A neighbor purchased a newer computer and asked me if would like to have her old one for free. Gee! Gosh! I was afraid of the thing - too old to learn new tricks.

All of my close neighbors were willing to help; Bob Colby, Lon Eason, Ben Cravey, Mary Garnto, my grandson Seth Senkbeil, and anyone I came in contact with. I had no instruction manual so I checked books out of the library and became even more confused. Finally it was passable and I showed it to my printer Randy Landers, at Fast Copy. He did a great job of formatting it for me.

Then it was time to find someone to do illustrations of the things I talked about in my book. Lance Coalson of Father & Son Publishing, introduced me to his niece Jessica Coalson, who became my illustrator. Jessica is a student at Darton College in Albany, Georgia. She drew all the things I asked her to, and even helped put them into the book.

So many people have helped me. Look and see.

Table of Contents

About the Author

I was born in Worth County, Georgia in 1928. I was number three of four children: girl, boy, girl, boy. We always lived in the community where I was born. We were taught to do whatever was needed to help our family survive with the resources available to us.

This story tells about these years in a way I hope you can relate and remember if you are about my age.

At this point in my life, I am the only survivor of my immediate family. There are two wives of my brothers' still living, as well as nieces and nephews of my three siblings. I am a widow now. My husband died in 2009.

My husband and I had wanted children for so long. After many miscarriages, several doctors told us that we could not have children. We then proceeded to travel the road of adoption. This was not an easy road to travel. Just when we were about to give up, a beautiful seven-month-old baby boy became available to us. We were happy and so was he. The next year, we gave birth to our beautiful miracle child. He was an eight pound, five and a half ounce boy. A miracle! Two years later, we adopted our precious little girl. Nine years later, we were able to adopt our adorable third son. Oh, those happy years! Gone, but not forgotten.

My wonderful family is still growing. I have thirteen grandchildren, four step-grandchildren, six great grandchildren, and one step-great grandchild.

Memories are what we older generation have to keep us happy and busy.

CHAPTER 1
HOME

The sun just coming up over the trees in the cow pasture... giving a promise of a clear hot day... just what the farmers need at this season of the year. Lots of work to be done before harvesting the crops begins.

Living on the farm, the only life I had ever known and now to remember so many things—like the sun, just coming up over the cow pasture—is such a pleasure! Remembering how we were told the earth is round and others have seen this same sun shining long before we have, on this same day—wow! Trying to figure out how people can do as we do, on a round world. How can we do things we do on what we feel is a "flat" world?

Early in the mornings when the sun is just rising, there is usually a small but sometimes a large, amount of 'dew'. It is wet but not like rain. It does make bare feet sticky and sandy, to be tracked into the house. The sight of the fresh sunlight and the dew makes everything look new. Sometimes Daddy or Mama would be humming a song or even one of us children, to make the day start off good! Trying to wake up, hearing the rooster crowing and Daddy grunting as he puts on his overalls and drops his shoes with a bang, knowing he will have to 'reach' for them, grunting again. That night he had been so tired, he let me take his shoes off of his tired feet. Mama had a pan of water with Epsom salts for him to soak his feet and I was allowed to rub them. Sometimes my two brothers also liked to do this. If Daddy was not too tired, he would blow his harp for us while we washed his feet.

Later, Daddy would build a place by the smokehouse where we would be able to take a shower. Two poles were placed about four feet from the smokehouse and four feet from each of the poles. A cotton sheet would be hung on wire stretched around the post to the smokehouse, and we would use clothespins to attach the cotton sheets and have privacy to have a shower bath. A tub of water would be drawn up and put near the side of the shower so one could dip a bucket of water, warmed by the sun. There was a special place for the bucket to hang while we had our bath. This bucket would have holes, in the bottom that had been hammered with nails, to let the water drip down as slowly as possible, while we took a bath. Before we had the shower, we used a washtub to get an all over bath. We used a pan and washcloth and Mama's home made soap to take a bath. We were made to wash our feet before going to bed! We had to always dress before we left our room—no one was allowed to run around the house in his or her underclothes.

Every day, Mama got up and started a fire in the cooking stove before calling each of us to begin the morning chores. We got our milk pails and put some water in them, along with some cloths Mama had placed in a basket in the kitchen for us to wash the cows' bags and 'tits' with before we began milking. One of the first things we were taught before being allowed to help with the milking was to wash the cows' bag and 'tits' first. The cows had been in the pasture or in the cow pen all night and had been, lying down, so it was necessary to wash the cows' bag and 'tits'. We were told to always go on the right side of a cow and had to pat her hind leg to make her "back it up" for us to start the milking process.

Milk was one of the most important food items in our family. I remember hearing Mama and Daddy talking about the time I cried for milk, once when our cows were not being milked! Daddy borrowed a cow from a neighbor that had several that were being milked at that time. To be able to have a cow that 'gives' milk, the cow has to have had a baby calf. Many of my little friends when I was little did not know this.

Living on the farm and being part of a farm and all that goes on at the farm was so different when girls were not allowed to be "in on things" that were happening on the farm every day. For a baby of any kind to be born, the male and female had to have been together. This was "God's decision" and is proper. All farmers did not have a bull (male cow) on their farm but most seemed to have a milk cow. Those that did not have a male would carry the female cow to visit the farm that did own a bull. Some farmers charged for this service but some were just good neighbors. Most people shared whatever they had with their neighbors, to help them to make a better living. Most figured they could be next to need help!

My job was to milk Nancy and Sally. Once, Nancy had a new baby calf that was just learning to hobble and was so cute. I had not given it a name yet. I got a bucket of feed and put it in Nancy's stall. I let her in the stall and got a large bucket to sit on. I sat down on 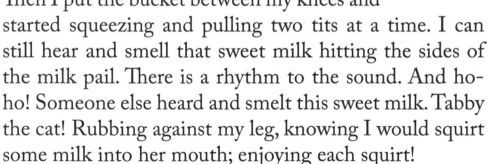 her right side to wash her bag, 'tits' and dry them. Nancy was busy eating and did not mind that I was washing her bag and 'tits'. Then I put the bucket between my knees and started squeezing and pulling two tits at a time. I can still hear and smell that sweet milk hitting the sides of the milk pail. There is a rhythm to the sound. And ho-ho! Someone else heard and smelt this sweet milk. Tabby the cat! Rubbing against my leg, knowing I would squirt some milk into her mouth; enjoying each squirt!

Nancy turned her head and looked at me with those big brown eyes and switched her tail as if to say, "that's enough of that!" When I finished with Nancy, I set the pail of milk on a shelf and covered the pail to keep flies and anything else, like cats, out of the milk.

Cats are a necessary part of farm life. They are usually at the barn. With all the feed that is stored there, rats soon would take over if it weren't for them. Our cats were able to keep at least part of the population down. However, sometimes the cat population became a problem and we had to find homes for the extra cats. Neighbors were glad to get one or more of the kittens while they were small. We usually had one or two that stayed near the house, but never in the house.

Our dogs and cats around the house tried to get along. The cats at the barn stayed away from the dogs.

Now it was time to allow the new baby calf in to the stall with Nancy. It came warbling and tripping as fast as it could go to get to the tits and started sucking with all of its might. There was lots of white foam around its mouth. Ummmmmmm Good!

Next it was Sally's turn to be milked. Her calf was much older and I would need to leave more milk in her bag for him. His name was Sammy and he was so strong. I go through the same routine with Sally as with Nancy. When it's time to let Sammy in to Sally, I had to be extra careful, or he would knock me down. When he got to Sally he would turn his rear end to her head and she would switch her tail around to touch him. She would turn her head and lick his back hip —this is to say, "Hello, little one. I love you!" (Cow language!)

The boys had finished their cows and taken the milk in the house to Mama and they would go back to separate the cows and the calves. The calves had a special pen and the cows had a fenced in lane to carry them to the woods to a pasture to spend the day. I took the milk from Nancy and Sally in to Mama and told her which pail of milk was from Nancy. She took a cup and dipped into this and tasted it and said," No, we will not be able to use it yet. Nancy's calf is still too young. In a few days it will be good for us to use." She handed Daddy this pail of milk to carry to the pigs and they would enjoy it. Mama would strain the other milk through a cloth and put this in a pan or a bowl. Then it would be set it in the icebox and a skim of cream would form on this milk. She would skim this cream off and put it in a baked clay urn that we would churn until butter formed. The churn was about two feet high and had a lid with a small round hole in it. A handle fit through this hole, and on the end of this handle were two short flat blades of wood that were crossed. When this handle was moved many times up and down, the butter formed and Mama would dip this from the milk and wash it several times before getting out her butter mold. The butter mold was similar to the churn, but much smaller. About the size of a small coffee cup, this mold had a round wooden disk at the end of the handle, with flower leaves engraved on the underside of it. Butter would be dipped into the cup (held with the handle at the bottom open part of the cup). When held up, it was filled with butter, which was packed down. The cup was turned over on wax paper and the handle pressed down to allow the butter to leave the cup.

Mama would then fold the wax paper over the butter and place it in the icebox. We had lots of butter. Mama took it to town on Saturdays and sold the butter, cream and eggs at the store that bought these from the farmers' wives each week. She gave us our allowance of 25 cents each to go to the moving picture show to see a Wild West movie —maybe Roy Rogers, Dale Evans, and Trigger (Roy's horse). After the movie, we would check in with Mama and she would let us walk around the streets, but we were never to go into the stores unless one of them (Mama or Daddy) was with us. We met new friends this way and hoped to see them the next week.

Mama would have breakfast ready for us, when we finished our chores. I liked to watch Mama cook. Maybe, someday I'd be able to help her more. She fixed biscuits, sausage, eggs and butter to put in our biscuits. The syrup and the honey were on the table. We children drank milk and Mama and Daddy drank Hot Coffee! Coffee was not good for us, they told us!

Daddy made our table. It was about ten feet long and has benches on each side. Mama sat at the end in a chair. Daddy sat at Mama's right side and I sat at her left side. The boys sat on either side of Daddy or me. At, mealtime we waited until we were all seated and Daddy said the blessing. He asked God's blessing for our food and for each one of us, and then he talked to God about anything else he wanted to mention. The food was on the table and we were to say, "pass" whatever we wanted, and, "thank you" to the person that passed our food to us.

To leave the table, for any reason, we had to say, "Excuse me, or May I, be excused, please?" We were not allowed to reach and grab what we wanted. We enjoyed our time spent together. We may have been tired or grumpy, but we could not show this at the table.

I remember the first time I saw Big Granny, Daddy's mama, put syrup onto her plate over butter and stir this and then beat it with a fork until it foamed. She would then put some on her biscuit, smack her lips together and say, "Ummmmmm Good!" (After this, I wanted mine like hers).

The well was out the back door, between the house and the barn. We had to tote buckets of water, for the cows, mules, and hogs. To draw and tote the water was a long hard job. Daddy decided to do something about this. He built a sluice of long planks, nailing them together to reach a barrel at the barn. The planks were thin and nailed together in such a way as to let the water run downward from the well. He used raw turpentine to seal the 'V' shaped planks so the water would not drip through and more would go into the barrel. This meant now we could dip the water from the barrel and not have to tote it so far to the troughs. Drawing the water from the well and pouring it from the bucket to the sluice was fun. It sure saved many steps.

One morning when we finished breakfast, Daddy said it

was time to go to the crib to get some corn ready to take to the mill. He and the boys went on and I stayed to help Mama wash the dishes and empty the slop jar.

We were not allowed to go outside at night. There might be a wild animal or stray dogs outside, or a convict might be loose. So we used the slop jar at night to "go to the bathroom." It had a lid on it and was under Mama and Daddy's bed. We had to be very quiet and not wake Daddy when we had to "use" the slop jar. We had a special place to empty the slop jar away from the house between the house and the tobacco barn. It had to be washed out and hung on the fence post to dry out before bringing in at night.

After I helped Mama wash the dishes and empty the slop jar, she had some sewing she needed to do and was busy with this. So, I went to help Daddy and the boys with the corn. As I reached the barn door, my older brother yelled, "Here! I've got a present for you." And he threw a mouse at me. I screamed and Daddy laughed and the mouse got away. We shucked the dry shucks from the ears of corn and placed the best shucks in a sack for Mama to use to redo her scrub mop. We had a neat pile of corn done when Daddy said that was enough for now. He got the corn Sheller and the long box he had built to hold the grains of corn down from where he had stored it. The Sheller, a metal tool with a handle to turn, was placed on the box. The Sheller had a place to feed the ears of corn and as the handle turned, the grains of corn fell into the box. The cobs were put into a corner of the cribs to be carried to the woodpile to be burned next wash day, around the wash pot. Some were taken to the toilet, to use as we did, with catalog pages.

I held the sack while Daddy poured the grains of corn into it and then he tied the sack with a piece of wire, to keep it from spilling. Next time he went to town, he would take this to the mill to have it ground into corn meal. Mama used lots of corn meal, making the corn bread we ate with our vegetables. We slept really good after a hard day's work and a big bowl of corn bread soaked in sweet milk. Mama's corn bread was good enough to eat by itself! She would put the meal into a mixing bowl, add baking soda, lard, and an egg. She would then add milk to this and stir and beat it until she felt it was just right to hold in her hands. She took a lump of the mixture in her hands and rocked it back and forth, until it formed a "pone-of-corn bread." She would place the pone in a big baking pan she had greased with lard, to keep it from sticking. There could be as many as six big pones of this bread, in the pan. She would put this into the hot oven and, when it was a pretty brown, she would remove it from the oven. Yes! Mighty Good.

I can't remember if Daddy or Granddaddy made our icebox. It was opened at the top to load the ice in. The "Ice man" came twice a week. The icebox would hold one hundred pounds of ice and, if we had the money, we would buy from him. He came in an old pick-up truck.

We would cover the ice with an old quilt, wrap it around it real tight, and close the lid of the icebox. At the bottom of the icebox would be two steel shelves, to keep the milk and butter cold. There were times that we did not get ice, and Daddy would let the bucket down in the well with the milk and butter or cream to keep them cold. The well water was always cold.

There seemed to be something always needing to be done. Daddy built our outhouse. We had needed one for so long! I would run errands for Daddy, to get what he wanted me to get nails, boards, saw, or hammer. I was glad to be his helper. Our outhouse was quite large and had two places to sit (Mamas had to assist children sometimes.) On the side, from the door, he fixed a place to hold an old catalog. This was used as toilet paper. There was a large bucket on the other side for used paper to be put in, and this would be burned later. Also a place was made to hold the corncobs, when available. We were very proud of our outhouse. We did not have to find a hiding place (a weed, stick or something to use after doing whatever we had to do) anymore when we had to "go." The new outhouse had a string for lifting the latch from inside, when privacy was needed, and no one would come in on us at this time.

We very seldom wore shoes, and we tracked lots of dirt in on our feet. Mama made the brooms she swept the floor with. These were made of straw that grew along the road, or at the edge of the fields. We would go with Mama when she went to get the straw. She took a sharp knife to cut it with. The straw grew about four feet high and she would cut them down near the bottoms. The tops were a little bushy. When we got to the house with these, she had a knife she used to trim the sharp sides from the straw. Then, with a string, she would wrap around the bottom part of these straws to hold them together, leaving the upper part bushy to sweep with. This broom was used many times a day, as we children were always going in and out, and our bare feet seemed to carry dirt into the house.

Once I went in to see if Mama had finished a dress she was making for me, and if, she was ready for me to try it on. She would need to pin it around the bottom, to hem it. Mama looked out the window where she had heard a sound, and there was a wagon pulling into the yard.

"Run and tell Daddy, we've got company," she said. Daddy and my brothers had also heard this and were going out to meet the "company." They were Daddy's Cousin Lawson and Cousin Annie. They lived down the road from us and were our neighbors. We were always glad to see them. They had many tales to tell and they both used tobacco in ways we did not see our folks use it. Cousin Lawson used chewing tobacco. This is a tobacco that has been processed and pressed into a small package. He took a bite off, and put it in one side of his mouth and every once in a while would need to spit the juice from this. He carried a "spit cup" with him, to use in the house.

Outside he would just spit on the ground. Cousin Annie dipped snuff, and she carried her snuff in a little round tin can that had a top to fit the can. She would pull her bottom lip out and pour this processed powdered tobacco in between her teeth and lip. She also brought her "spit cup" with her, to use in the house.

Cousin Annie, Mama and I went in the house to start cooking dinner. Cousin Annie had said, they had come to spend the day. Mama already had butter beans with a ham hock cooking, for we had shelled the butter beans the night before. She sent me to the garden to get tomatoes and okra, and I took a spoon to dig some Irish potatoes (making sure to cover the place where I dug the potatoes out, so they will keep producing.) Then, I was sent to the corn patch to get six ears of corn (making sure to look at the silks and be sure they were turning brown and would be ready to use).

Mama was doing so many things and Cousin Annie was busy peeling and slicing the tomatoes, and they were having fun, laughing and talking. Mama, told me to take the corn out on the porch to shuck it and get the silks off. Then she told me to get the pan and some water and go back on the porch and scrape the skins off the potatoes, using a spoon, to do this. I wondered what meat we were having, as she had not told me to go get a chicken and wring its neck. Then I smelled the wonderful odor of fried ham. Yes, so good! Smoked fried ham! Mama must have already been to the smokehouse to get this. She had several eggs boiling and the potatoes were cooking. I was told to go to the smokehouse and get a jar of pickle cucumbers that she had canned earlier this year. Then I set the table. Daddy and Cousin Lawson moved the table from the wall when they came in. We had some ice, in the icebox and Mama was chipping off enough to go in the glasses. So I knew we were having iced tea. Mama used an ice pick to chip the ice. The table was ready and all of us had a place to sit and eat together. Sometimes, when there were extra people at the table, the children had to wait to eat until the grown-ups were finished. When this happened, there were usually other children with the company, and we'd go outside to play. We didn't mind waiting. Daddy either asked the blessing or he may ask a guest to do it. On this visit, he asked the blessing. So much food on the table! Ham with raised gravy (water put in the grease and cooked with the meat); potato salad with pickles and boiled eggs, onions and butter; okra and tomato soup, and okra battered and fried crispy; butter beans with ham hocks; corn (scraped from the cob) boiled and thickened; cornbread and biscuits; cucumber pickles, and sliced tomatoes. The syrup, honey and butter were always on the table. Everyone was eating, laughing and talking. After the meal, Daddy, the boys and Cousin Lawson went to the front porch to stretch out and rest. Daddy always got a little nap. Mama, Cousin Annie and I did the dishes, and put away the food. The scraps were saved to give to the cats and chickens later. A table full of good things to eat! "Company's coming" and we had fun!

CHAPTER 2
QUILTING

I remember one time when Big Granny, Daddy's mama, was visiting us. She wore her hair long and pulled back from her face and I loved to watch her "dress" her hair. She would comb it through with a big comb and then rub it with her hands and pull it over her shoulder, twist it until she had it like a rope, and then wind it around itself at the nap of her neck until it was in a neat little ball. She used large hairpins, to hold it together and in place. Then, she would wet her hands and rub the front part of her hair until all the loose hair was melded into the other hair. This helped make it stay in place. Big Granny always wore long dresses and high top shoes and stockings. Her apron bib hung around her neck and waist, and tied by strings or belt of the same material, as the apron tied in the back. The apron had big pockets and she carried many things in them. Her snuffbox was one and her spit cup was always near. She might have a pretty little rock she had picked up, a bird feather, or her little knife that she used for many things, even to clean under her fingernails. She might have a dried flower or a brush that she would make from a sassafras vine. She always came prepared to make us a brush like hers. Bringing many short sassafras lengths of vine in her pocket, she would peel off a small end of the short vine. Then, she would cut around the end and chew on the peeled end until it became a little brush. We would all watch her make these and be happy to get one.

I had figured out why she came to visit us this time. I remembered that I had heard Cousin Annie and Mama talking about the Quilting party they were planning. Big Granny had the tools needed to pull the seed from the cotton that Mama would need to go in the quilt. Mama and I had been cutting and sewing small pieces of cloth together to make a pattern for the top of the quilt for a long time. It was Mama's way of teaching me how to sew.

We had gone to the cotton field last week and picked the scattering cotton left by the people picking the cotton. We had enough to go between the top and bottom of a quilt. Big Granny used her tools to get the black, cottonseed, out of the lint. The black seed had sharp edges that stuck like pins in ones fingers. The tools were two brushes, like a hair brush, except the bristles were longer, and they were larger than her hands. She would take a small amount of cotton and put it between the brushes and pull and push until the black seed came out. The lint was then ready to be put in the bottom part of the quilt, on the frame (thinly).

Daddy had been hard at work preparing for the quilting. He had put the meat hanging hooks in the ceiling to hold the chains that would hold the frame and the bottom part of the quilt. Granddaddy had made the frames for Big Granny, and she let Mama use them. There were four pieces of the frame. Each piece had holes bored in them to help hold the material in place while the quilt was being made. Each person would have a place to sit in a half circle, and they would mark where they should start quilting with white chalk. This was rolled, so the next row could be done. This went on and on, until the quilt was finished. Women in the community were told about the quilting and were glad to be a part of it. They would be having one soon, and people were glad to be invited. They had fun talking about what was going on in the community, exchanging recipes, and deciding who would have her pieces ready for the next quilting party! Most of the women that came to the quilting had children and they came to the quilting, too.

The older children helped watch after the younger ones and all enjoyed playing many games. The boys liked to play marbles. The girls like to jump rope and they all liked to play hide and go seek. Hopscotch and a ball game were always enjoyed. Mama had baked a cake and made some cookies, so there was food to eat and plenty of sweet milk or buttermilk to drink. It had been a day when "Company came," and we had fun!

After everyone was gone, it was time to clean up.

The quilt was taken from the frame and Mama and Big Granny were hemming it to be ready to put on a bed when needed. The quilt was so pretty, and years from now these same women could see the quilt and tell just where they had done the sewing on it. The table had to be put back in place, extra chairs that had been borrowed had to be returned to the neighbors, dishes used for the party at refreshment time had to be washed and put away. Then it was time to take Big Granny home. We would load the quilting frames and all the things she had brought with her on the truck, and be on our way. We would not get to stay long at her house, as we had to get home and do the night chores.

CHAPTER 3
TOBACCO BED

After the quilting party was over and the chores were finished, Mama and Daddy talked at supper about what they needed to do now. At the right season of the year, Daddy would always go to the woods and start looking for a place to put the tobacco bed. He would look for the tool he had made to measure space, as he wanted to use it to measure where he would put the tobacco bed. If he could not find it, then he would have to make another one. To make the tool, he needed three tobacco sticks. He knew how to make it, as he wanted it to turn and to measure the width and length of the bed. It would look like a big 'A' with some of the tops of the sticks poking out at the top and a shorter piece about mid-way. This held the pieces exactly where he needed them to be, which was about three feet apart. He would count the number of times he twirled the sticks around and write this number down in the book he carried in his overall bib pocket. Both the length and the width had to be measured, and staked off at this point, so that when he brought the mules down to plow the grass up, he would know where to work. Tobacco sticks were used to hang tobacco in the barn to be either cured or cooked. After the tobacco leaves were put on these narrow sticks, they were still green. The sticks measured four feet, four inches long, and were one inch thick and very strong. We found many ways to use these sticks. It took many of these sticks to fill a tobacco barn with tobacco leaves. After selecting a spot to make the tobacco bed, Daddy selected four trees to be cut down. Two were for the length of the bed and two were for the width of the bed. These had to be sawed down and trimmed of the small limbs, branches and tops of the trees. After they lay awhile, they were skinned. The bark of the tree had to be taken off to keep insects from nesting in it.

Daddy and Mama used a two-handed saw to cut the trees down, and an ax and single-handed saw to cut the branches and top off. The trees stayed where Daddy cut them down until he was ready to put them around the bed.

The mule and plow would be taken to the spot he had chosen, and Daddy would plow the tough grass up. We helped pull and tug these bunches of grass to a place he would tell us, and, when it dried, he burned them. He would work this bed many times to rid it of the grass and grass seeds before he would be ready to put the logs around it. When it came time to bring the logs to the bed, Daddy would take the mule and a chain to hook around each log  to pull the logs in place around the bed. He notched the logs with a saw and the logs would be attached to each other so they would not roll away. He still worked the ground between these logs, keeping the earth soft. At the right time (he and Mama decided this), Daddy got the small can of tobacco seed and scattered them evenly on top of this soft ground, over the entire bed. Then he had a board that had been nailed on the end of a tobacco stick to use to press these tiny seeds into the soft ground.

Sometimes when he was packing the seed in the ground, he would ask us to get in the tobacco bed with him to use our bare feet to pack the earth and seed together. All, this work had to be done in an orderly way and, as he cut the tree branches and tops off, we had to put these in a certain place for Daddy to burn when the weather would be just right, not too wet or windy.

Also when he skinned the trees, the shavings had to be cleaned up for burning too. Next, he had to cover the bed with a cloth to keep the wild animals off the bed. He had to tack this cloth on the logs all around the bed, keeping the cloth up and off the seed.

Mama would send or bring us a snack while we were

helping Daddy, maybe some gingerbread, fresh from the oven with some buttermilk to drink. Daddy would always smack his lips together and tell her how good these snacks were. We never failed to thank her too.

Daddy was always working, getting things done. I remember how wet his clothes were with sweat, and a white substance that Mama said was salt from his body (sweat). Did he ever work hard!

When the tobacco seed begin to show tiny leaves above the ground, Daddy would lift the cloth to let the sun shine in on the little plants. He'd have to be real careful and watch during the time the cloth was off, for the little wild animals and birds liked to explore and see what was going on.

As the plants grew, so did the grass and we helped him pull weeds from around the little plants. We had to be careful and not step on any of the tiny plants and not pull any up with the grass.

CHAPTER 4
TOBACCO TRANSPLANTING

Daddy knew when it was time to transplant the tobacco to the field. He knew where he would be, preparing this land for the plants. He and Mama had talked it over and he would be ready to start.

The land had to be turned, and then the rows had to be banked and fertilized and ready to transplant the tobacco plants. He also would need the transplanter checked out to. This was an aluminum cylinder tool, with a sharp end on the bottom that opens, like a mouth. When guided and twisted, a spring was released to let the water and the plant drop into the hole made with the sharp end. The larger part of the cylinder held the water, and the smaller tube beside it was hollow and this was where the plant was placed and dropped down into the hole with the water, to be covered by someone

following behind the person with the transplanter.

At the proper time, we would get up early in the morning and go to the tobacco bed to pull the plants that were big enough to transplant.

We were very careful not to break the roots of the plants, as they will not live if the roots are broken. The plants were placed in a washtub with a little water in it to keep the roots from drying out while we were planting the others. These plants were taken to the field that Daddy had ready for them to be transplanted in. Daddy would use the transplanter and Mama would be the one to walk backward, dropping the plants into the cylinder. My older brother would be the one to come back of the transplanted plants to be sure the roots were down, and to cover and pack the soil around the plant so it can grow. I would be the one to tote the water and plants to Daddy and Mama, as they needed them. My little brother would be at the water barrel and have a bucket of water filled for me to take back to them, as they needed it. We would take a short break and have a snack at mid-morning. And then in about no time, we would break for dinner.

Mama and I would go to the house to finish getting dinner on the table. Daddy and the boys had to add some water to the barrel and to the plants. Mama would have prepared most of the dinner as she fixed breakfast, so dinner would be ready quickly. Mama would get tired from walking backwards to drop the plants in the planter, so I helped her as much as I could with dinner and cleaning up afterwards. If we had enough plants to plant the entire field that Daddy had prepared, it would be great, but if not, then in a day or two there would be plants that were big enough to finish this field.

It would usually be cool when we got started early in the morning pulling the plants, but up in the day it got hot. Earlier, we appreciated the long sleeves we had on and later when the sun got hot, we still appreciated the long sleeves, which kept our skin from burning.

The little spindly plants would be watched carefully by Daddy and any grass that dared to come up near the plants had to be hoed up. Daddy had the mule hitched to a plow to throw dirt near the plants and help keep the grass away. The plants would grow tall and fast. Soon, they would have a tassel on the top. The leaves would get wider, and between the leaves and the stalks, a small growth would appear. These were called suckers. We would have to break off the tassel and pinch off the sucker or- as Daddy said-the sucker would soon suck all the juice from the tobacco. The rows of tobacco had to be hoed and plowed several times. Soon, it would be time to crop the tobacco. A lot of work had to be done before Daddy could be ready for cropping the tobacco.

CHAPTER 5
TOBACCO BARN

The barn had to be ready. It was a tall square barn back of the house, and had four smoke stacks sticking out of its roof. The tobacco barn had tiers that were so many feet apart and reached the top of the barn. This is where the sticks of green tobacco were hung to cook.

The furnace that heated the barn had to have lots of wood ready for cooking the tobacco. Sometimes the neighbors helped Daddy and the boys go to the woods and cut down the trees and get the wood ready to bring to the barn. They would help stack a tall stack of this wood near the barn. The barn had  a shelter on one side of it, and the shelter had a shelf as long as the shelter. It would hold the green tobacco, when it was placed on the shelf to be handed to the one to string it on a tobacco stick. If there were not enough tobacco sticks, Daddy would go to the sawmill and have some more made. They had to be four feet and four inches long, and one-inch square to fit in the tiers of the barn for cooking.

CHAPTER 6
TOBACCO SLED

The sled had to be rebuilt one season. A tobacco sled had to be narrow enough to go between the rows of tobacco, in the field. The sled was on runners that made it easy for the mules to pull slowly, as the croppers put the leaves into the sled. The sled had burlap sacks that had been split apart and nailed around all the insides of the sled to keep from bruising the leaves.

The croppers had two rows each to crop the leaves and place into the sled. The stems must always be toward, the middle of the sled. When placed on the shelf at the barn, the leaves must have the stems pointing to the inside of the barn, to make it easy for the ones handing the tobacco leaves to the stringer (three leaves at a time). The croppers took only 'ripe' leaves from each stalk.

String Horse

Sometimes the string horse had to be remade. The string horse was made with a wide board, not quite as long as the tobacco stick -maybe a foot shorter. Enough room had to be left on each end of the stick to hang on the tiers in the barn, so the leaves would hang free. Another board about four feet tall and six inches wide, a smaller one, leaned to brace this board at each end. Each top end of these boards would have a 'V' shape notched in it, to hold the stick in place while the stringer strung the tobacco on the stick.

A can was nailed to the stick horse, to hold the strong twine needed to wrap around the hand of three leaves of tobacco on either side of the stick. Maybe the old stick horse just needed new nails  to tighten and straighten it, to make it ready to be in use again.

CHAPTER 7
TOBACCO GATHERING

Now, word was sent to the neighbors, to see if any were free to help with the gathering of the tobacco. A day would be set for them to come - and if needed - to bring an extra string horse from their house.

On this day, Mama cooked a big meal for dinner, as all the help would be staying to eat. "Company's coming" for real! And everyone would be hungry!

The mules were hitched to the sleds and ready when everyone got to the tobacco barn. At least two string horses were used. Two people would string the tobacco on the tobacco sticks, and four people would hand the tobacco to those that wrapped the strings around the hands of tobacco - three leaves at the time. The mules pulled the sleds to the shelf and someone would lift the leaves out of the sled and place them, with the stems pointed inside, on the shelf. Now the workers at the barn would begin to race with each other, to see who could get the first stick of tobacco strung and hung in the barn. This was "part of the fun" as everyone was laughing and teasing each other.

The leaves of the tobacco were gritty and gummy, and everyone was dirty and came prepared. They knew this was how it was, and the work goes on. There could be ten to twelve people at the barn working, plus four croppers with the mules and sleds. Someone would tell a joke or start singing a song, (that everyone knows) and everyone would be laughing while they worked.

Mama would have one of us to ring the dinner bell to let the ones in the field know to come to the house for dinner. The workers would wash off some of the grim and sticky gummy stuff that sticks to the hands. Some of Mama's homemade soap and watermelon rind or some tomatoes may be ready to use,  to clean up before eating. As many as could, would sit at the table to eat. Others may get their plate fixed and find a place to sit either on the ground or a box or anywhere they can find to be comfortable while they ate. A short break after eating was again enjoyed. Some stretched out on the porch, or even on the ground, just to rest.

A tap on the dinner bell let everyone know when it was time to get back to work. The croppers should be finished in about two hours, and would come to help finish at the barn. Everyone was tired, but proud of what had been done.

The barn would be almost full on all the tiers and some might be rearranged to get the heat to all of the sticks better. Some would express their thoughts on how this should be done, in a friendly, joking way. Daddy would bring out the watermelons he had cooling in a tub of cold water, ready to be sliced and there was lots of salt ready, if anyone wanted to sprinkle it on their slices.

To make this a fun time, someone would start spitting the watermelon seeds, and the fight would begin... all in fun!

Most everyone would be ready to go home now, as it would soon be chore time. Daddy had seen that everything was tidy around the barn and closed the door for the night.

The barn of tobacco was allowed to "rest."

CHAPTER 8
TOBACCO COOKING

The next day, was the day to start the fire in the furnace, and from then on-until the tobacco was cured- someone would be sitting day and night with the barn, to keep the temperature going up or down, as needed.

On about the third night, after the tobacco had been cooking, a few friends and neighbors would just happen to come by, to see how things were going. Some brought their guitars, fiddles or harps, and the fun would begin. All ages would be there. No one had to be invited; it was just a custom. Mama would bake a cake and have a churn or two of ice cream ready to be churned. This had to be in a wooden bucket especially made for the churn. It had a top to the round cylinder part that held the ice cream mix in, and a handle that fit this top. Ice was packed around the cylinder and, as the handle turned, the ice would make the ice cream mix freeze. Oh Boy! Good! Singing, laughing, eating, and just fun!

Peanuts, in the wash pot, had been cooking all afternoon and were ready to eat. We had picked them off the vines and Mama put some salt in the water as they boiled and now they were cool enough to hold in one's hands to eat. The hull, was spit out, or thrown down on the ground. It was all right.

Some of the men were smoking or chewing their tobacco and some of the women were dipping their snuff, if they wanted to. Couples would slip off down the road to walk, and be alone with each other—and maybe steal a kiss or two.

Quilts appeared, and the smaller children were allowed to lay down and take a nap -if they could with all the noise. Young children were busy telling on each other for hitting someone, playing a game of marbles or wrestling. This would go on and on until Daddy called, "Bed time!" Everyone would be ready to go home and to bed.

All this time, Daddy had his eyes on the temperature and how the barn of tobacco was doing. He made sure there was enough wood available for the one who had to sit the rest of the night, as he had his work laid out for him. When Daddy decided the tobacco had cooked long enough, he would tell us, and no one would have to sit with the barn now. The fire was allowed to go out and the ashes would be removed from the furnace.

The barn door and the windows at the top of the barn were opened, to cool the barn and the tobacco down. Many barns had been left not tended to like Daddy did, and they would burn down and lose all this the hard work and all the tobacco in the barn. When the barn had cooled down enough, it would be time to unload the barn. Neighbors would come and help. Someone would hand down a stick of tobacco to someone else, and they would pass it along to someone in the wagon, and it would be stacked until the wagon was filled. This would be taken

to one of our bedrooms that had been emptied for this tobacco to be placed in. The wagon would be unloaded, and would go back and forth, until all the tobacco was stacked in this room. The tobacco would be covered with burlap sheets, until it has "rested" enough to handle.

 The string horses would be brought to the house and we would unstring the tobacco sticks, packing the tobacco on other sheets, and throwing the sticks outside. They were stacked and ready for the next tobacco to go on this same route.

CHAPTER 9
TOBACCO GRADING

After all the tobacco has been unstrung, grading the tobacco would start. There would be three grades- best, better, and trash.

Daddy had put the dinner table where it could be used to put stacks of the tobacco on, and we would start grading it. One sheet would be for the best, another for the better, and one for trash. As each sheet was filled, Daddy would

tie the corners of the sheets together, and stack them on top of each other. There would be several gatherings of the tobacco and all would be handled in this way.

Tobacco Market

When the market opened, Daddy would take what we had ready, and sell it. We liked to go and hear the auctioneers do their chanting as people bought the tobacco at the market. Daddy would collect his check and we would go home and start all over.

At the end of the season, when all of the tobacco was sold, Mama would go with us to buy our shoes and school clothes. She bought material to make my underwear and dresses, and some pencils and paper for us to use at school.

CHAPTER 10
SPRING PLANTING

In the, Spring Time, or as soon as it begin to warm up after a cold spell, Daddy would begin to get his plows ready to "turn" or "break" the land where he intended to plant certain crops. Any stalks left from the crops of the year before had to be gathered and stacked to burn. Only when the wind was right could we do the burning. Sometimes a whole field would be burned off before the field could be plowed, to be sure and get rid of unwanted grass and stalks.

Then it was time to get the mules ready to hitch to the plow, and begin to turn the soil up and get rid of roots from grass and other things that showed sign of growing. There had to be time to allow the earth to "rest" before the actual planting began.

CHAPTER 11
COTTON PLANTING

Daddy would use his home made measuring sticks, to measure how he wanted the cotton rows to be planted. He had saved some cottonseed from the last year's crop, but he could buy a new type of cottonseed to plant. He would have to decide and get some before planting time.

I was kept out of school to help with the planting. My older brother helped Daddy and got things ready to go to the field. Fertilizer and seed in the wagon was placed at the ends of the rows to be planted. My job was to keep buckets filled and ready to take to the planting plows, as needed. Sometimes, I would have time to play in the sand and if I had time, I slipped a library book to the field with me. Mama did not like this, as she was afraid the sunlight would hurt my eyes. I loved to read, and would hide my book when Daddy got near. Mama would bring us a snack and fresh water, about the middle of the morning. It was always so appreciated! The rows of cotton were always so long and straight. I never knew how Daddy could do this; it seemed a miracle to me.

When the seed begin to produce little plants with leaves, we had to hoe around each plant and get the grass to loosen the ground so the cotton could grow.

When we got in from school, we changed into our work clothes. There was always work to be done and we grabbed what we were allowed to eat and headed for the field.

It would soon be time to do the nighttime chores-feeding, watering and milking the cows, bringing in the fire wood and the slop jar, and washing up for supper. Mama would have supper on the table, left over from dinner, with lots of cornbread and milk, and fresh young onions from the garden.

After the dishes were washed and put away, we did our homework. The teacher knew we had to work when we got home from school, and did not overload us with homework.

Our folks were so proud that we went to school and would be better prepared to earn a living than they were. They did not expect us to make all 'A's...just to do our best.

When the cotton plants began to have little leaves and little blooms on them, Daddy would put some mixture of poison in a little cloth sack that Mama had made for him to use. He would sprinkle a little of this poison on each plant, on each row, and it would take a long time!

CHAPTER 12
FISHING

Daddy worked hard, but while he was working he was often thinking about taking us fishing. He would suggest we dig some worms for bait. He had already shown us where to look for the worms and their mounds of dirt (they dug deep in the ground to live). We would take a hoe and dig or a shovel to scoop under the mounds of dirt and pick up the worms. We put a small amount of dirt in the can for them to be in and stay alive, until where we were going to go fishing.

It was almost as much fun to dig for the worms, as it was to go fishing. There was more to getting ready to go fishing than just digging the bait. Everyone had to have a pole. On the pole, the line had a hook and a small piece of lead. Daddy used his pliers to squeeze the lead on tight, to weight the hook down as deep as he wanted it to go. A cork stopper (like we used on our syrup bottles) was threaded onto the line, and was then tied on the pole. If not enough poles were already fixed, Daddy would cut a gallberry limb long enough to use and attach a line he had already fixed. Then, everyone was happy.

We watched our corks to see if they would bobble, and if they did, it meant a fish could be nibbling on the worm placed on the hook. We were to pull the pole up and out, and, if there was a fish on the hook, Daddy will take it off. He had a short gallberry limb he had cut in just the

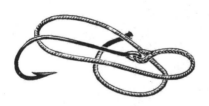 right place, and would thread this through the fish's mouth. The limb would be long enough so that Daddy could push the end of it down into the shallow

water, and the fish would stay alive until we were ready to go home. We hoped to catch lots of fish, so we could have fried fish for supper, with hot biscuits and lots of syrup.

We would go to the creek (we called it "Levi") in the wagon. Daddy would hitch the mules to a tree. We took plenty of water and food for us to stay for a while, should we get hungry or thirsty. Mama enjoyed going fishing too, so we were all there. If we used all the worms we had dug, he showed us how to "grunt" for more. We found a mound of dirt the worms had dug for their home, and stick a stick near this mound and rub another stick on top of this stick. Soon the worms would wiggle out of the ground and we would pick them up and put them in a can. For us, this is where the name "wiggle worm" came from.

We were told to be very quiet, and keep a look out for snakes or any other wild animals.

When anyone caught a fish of any size or even get a "bite" everyone got excited. Bream, perch, or any scale fish, had to have the scales scraped off. Catfish had to be skinned. Mama would then dip the fish in a pan of hot water and use a cloth to rub the fish with and the catfish skin came off on the cloth. All the fish had to be cut open and their insides taken out. When Mama cleaned the fish for cooking, the insides were given to the cats, and they loved these. We had to be home in time to do the chores, and while we were doing these chores, Mama dressed and cooked the fish for our supper.

CHAPTER 13
COTTON HOEING

Soon after cotton planting time, we had to hoe around each cotton plant. Daddy would sharpen the hoe with a file and this made the weeds and grass easier to cut off.

We always welcomed the rain. This meant we got to rest, after a Shower of rain. Sometimes it might hail during those showers, and this was bad for the crops, as it could tear them up. When the bowls begin to form from the blooms, we knew it would not be long before, cotton-picking time.

Cotton Picking

Mama and Daddy would begin to get things ready for cotton picking. There were long cotton sacks with straps to go around our neck for us to use for picking cotton. These were made out of thick material, as they were used to put the cotton that each one picked and pulled from the stalk. The sack was kept behind them as they pulled the cotton from the bowls of the stalk. Sheets had to be ready for pickers to empty their sacks on,

49

and these were the tobacco sheets used again. Those picking cotton, would bend way over, or crawl on their knees to pick the cotton. Most of those who crawled made kneepads, so the rocks would not hurt their knees as much. So they would not waste time going to eat at the house, pickers brought their dinner to the field. Some would bring their dinner in a bag or a tin box, to keep the ants from getting in. The more time they spent picking cotton, the more money they would make. At the end of the day, Daddy brought the mules hitched to the wagon, and the scales to weigh the cotton that each one picked. It required a long pole with the scales attached, and two people to lift the scales and the sheet of cotton to tell how much one picked in that sheet.

Daddy had a little book in his pocket and a pencil, and he wrote each name and the amount the scales said was in their sheet. The scales had a measuring yardstick that weighed up to three hundred pounds. Weights were shaped like little bells and made of iron, with a crooked piece at the top for the bell to hang onto the scale for weighing things. Weigh-up time was exciting. Everyone was interested to see who had picked the most cotton. Only hired help was paid. We family members knew this was just part of our chores. After weighing the cotton, the men helped Daddy load it on the wagon. Then at the house, the cotton was unloaded on the front porch and covered with a canvas, to keep the rain or dampness from soaking it. All the sheets were needed the next day, for the pickers to use. When enough cotton had been picked, it would be loaded onto the truck or wagon and hauled to the "gin."

CHAPTER 14
COTTON GIN / MARKET

The gin was a big metal building that had a covered shelter, for the farmers to drive their trucks or wagons under. A large tin pipe would be lowered down into the cotton and it would suck the cotton up into a place that would separate the seed from the lint, and then bundle the lint into a large bale. The farmer then got paid for his cotton and was allowed to buy seed too, if he desired.

Celebration time! Time to pay bills that had been made during the year, as had been promised.

CHAPTER 15
DINNER BELL

In the back yard, toward the tobacco barn, Daddy hauled a large pole and dug a deep hole with the whole digger. Mama helped him set it up, straight and he packed dirt tightly around it. On top of the pole, he built a place to hold the dinner bell. After the dirt settled and dried around the pole good, he used a ladder to climb to the top of the pole to attach the big black iron bell. It was so heavy, Mama held the ladder for him and handed him the rope to attach to the bell. The rope, would be used to make

the bell ring, when it was pulled. When the rope was pulled, the "clapper" -which was also made of iron and hung down loosely in the middle of the bell-hit the sides of the bell and rang, making lots of loud noise. The bell ringing let the workers know it was, "dinner time." At other times, when the bell was rung, it was a distress call for help. Most of the neighbors had dinner bells also, and recognized the sounds of each bell they heard ringing.

Children were taught early, "do not play with the rope!"

CHAPTER 16
PEANUTS

Peanuts meant a lot to our family. Daddy had special places he prepared on our land
for the different types of peanuts.
The runner types were mostly
planted in the cornfield, and
the Spanish was a bunch type
that was planted in long rows
in their designated field. Runner
peanuts were large and their
vines would run up the corn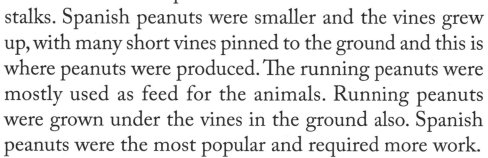
stalks. Spanish peanuts were smaller and the vines grew
up, with many short vines pinned to the ground and this is
where peanuts were produced. The running peanuts were
mostly used as feed for the animals. Running peanuts
were grown under the vines in the ground also. Spanish
peanuts were the most popular and required more work.

The mules were hitched to the plows, and the land
prepared to plant. The planter used for planting had a
hopper for peanuts on one side, and a hopper on the

other side for fertilizer. Again, I was required to help, by keeping a bucket of peanuts and fertilizer ready to take to the one using the planter as needed. The planter plowed the furrow with a sharp pointed blade, and the peanuts and fertilizer were spread in the furrow.

At the end of the plow, another part of the plow covered the furrow as it went on. It would take several days to complete the acreage that Daddy had in mind to plant. This was a family project and everyone worked hard.

Soon, little plants came up peeking through the soil, as did the weeds and grass. We would hoe the weeds and grass around each plant and Daddy would plow, throwing dirt near the peanut vines. We were careful not to cut down the vines. Little blooms came on the vines and the vines would spread, and Daddy would soon say that he would not be plowing them again because they needed the space in the middle of the row to pin down their vines and grow peanuts. Daddy would continue to watch and observe how big the peanuts were growing, and he would know when to be ready to harvest the peanuts.

Many things needed to be done first. He and the boys would go to the woods and cut down small pine trees and saw off their limbs and tops. They would then take a trip to the sawmill to get lumber to make the slats to nail on the bottom of the poles to be used to stack the peanuts on. The slats were about three feet long, and about four inches wide. A hole would be dug with hole-diggers, to place the poles in. The slats would be nailed onto the poles, to keep the peanuts off the ground during the curing time. Then

Daddy would begin plowing up the peanuts. We would start down each row and shake the dirt, from the vines of peanuts, and stack these in piles as we went. It was a dirty, tiring job.

After shaking and piling the peanut vines all day, or until we had enough piles of peanuts and vines to stack around the pole, Daddy would stack the peanuts. He would stack the peanuts on the inside of the stack and the vines would be on the outside of the stack. The pole would be topped with a bunch of grass. This was to keep the birds from getting the peanuts around the poles. The peanuts were allowed to cure for a while. In the meantime, Daddy would contact someone that had a peanut thrasher and a hay baler. He would get his name on the list, and would be told about when -according to the weather -they could be at our fields. Not many farmers had their own peanut thrashers or hay balers. The thrasher was a large machine, usually painted red, and was pulled by mules. On the inside were many wire-type fingers that constantly turned and pulled the nuts from the vines. The nuts fell into a special tray that shook anything small -like rocks and trash -out as the nuts went into a sack. They would then be emptied into a truck or a wagon standing ready to be hauled to the market when finished.

The vines had been beat off the nuts and were now considered hay. There was a machine pulled by a mule that would press these beat-up, crushed vines. The vines were put into the machine with pitchforks by men that worked for the owner of the machines and the hay would be pressed into bales. These bales would be tied with hay wire to hold the bales in place. These men would stack the bales to one side, and later the farmers would haul them to their barns to feed to their animals through the winter months. Daddy had built a special contraption, with runners and the bottom of a sled. He would back the mules to a stack of peanuts on the pole, and the runners would slide under the pole and lift the pole out of the ground and haul the stack to the thrasher.

Sometimes after the harvesting of the peanuts, we could invite a few friends and have a hayride. Daddy would load some scattering of the hay into the wagon and hitch the  mules to the wagon and he would drive the wagon and the mules.

We were excited and happy and our friends were too. We sang songs and laughed. Daddy sang with us and sometimes he would blow his harp. Mama would make a churn of ice cream and some cookies for our refreshments, to serve when we came back from the hayride. This was usually done after dark and everyone had to go home early, to go to work the next day.

Now the cows were allowed to go into the peanut field.

They had more room to roam and plenty to eat, and were ready to come into the barns at night to get lots of water to drink.

Now it was again celebration time! Time to pay bills and buy needed school clothes, if it had been a good crop year.

Parties were held during this season -peanut boiling, and proms, where boys and girls were allowed to walk down the road together. Many games were played to choose which girl or boy one would be walking with.

Peanuts were saved to plant for next year. These had to be shelled. Mama and Daddy would have a peanut shelling party, inviting several families and their children. We were each given a box of peanuts to shell and the one who finished their box first, got a prize. Maybe a dime! Daddy had made Mama a Peanut Sheller. He used two pieces of thin wood, about five inches long and an inch wide, and a piece of smaller wood was placed between these two wrapped pieces at the end she would hold in her hand. She would put a peanut in between the shafts of the Sheller and crack it open. This way she would not blister her fingers as she cracked the peanut shells.

During the winter months, as we sat around a fire before going to bed, we had a shoebox of peanuts to shell. This was just part of our chores.

CHAPTER 17
CORN

Spring brought lots of work to be done. Daddy had special places, or fields, he wanted to plant in corn. Some of these were in a part of the land that would be too wet at the regular planting season, to work. Using the same plows and planters he had used to plant other crops, hc put out seed and fertilizer to plant corn. At the same time, he would sometimes plant velvet beans. These beans were used as feed for the animals, along with the corn, according to his plan.

There was another type of corn, that we called, "roast-n-ary." We used this in our cooking, but we also used field corn. It was all very good to eat. Corn was used in so many ways. Mostly we took our corn to the mill that was set up for grinding the corn into very fine meal. Mama made lots of cornbread to go with our vegetables, or with milk. The mill was located near a stream of water that would turn the wheels to grind the corn. So, the meal was said to be "water ground."

Field corn was grown, mostly to make feed for the animals. Some was mixed with hay and velvet beans to make a variety of feed. The corn had to be looked after, like the other crops, and when weeds and grass came up in the rows, we knew it was time to use the hoe again. After hoeing the rows of corn, Daddy would plow it, throwing more soil up on the rows. As the corn grew taller, the roots would spread into the middle of the row, and Daddy would not plow it again. The tall corn had tassels at the tops of the stalks, and those roots grew big to hold the thin stalks with the heavy ears of corn that grew between the leaves and the stalk. Usually there were two or three ears of corn to a stalk, although some would only have one. These little shoots at first came between the stalk and leaf. Soon there would be little threads like silk poking out the end of the shoots. Then the shoots would turn into ears of corn, with many rows of grain on each ear. Just right for boiled corn on the cob with lots of salt. 'Wow! Good!'

At the end of the season, the ears of corn had dried in their shucks, and we would pull these dried ears of corn using the tobacco sled. We would haul the corn as we threw it into the sled. The mules were used to this noise and were very patient with us. We would haul these ears of corn to the crib and again throw them any 'ole' way into the place Daddy told us to. There was no way to stack them neatly in rows. We had fun throwing these ears of corn in the shucks. The shucks protected the grains of corn, so no damage was done. The shucks were removed from the corn when it was taken to the mill to grind into meal, grits or whatever.

Some of the green corn was sold to the stores in town, as everyone likes fresh corn. This corn would still have the green shucks and tassels on them.

The corn stalks grew very tall, and they would have to be cut down after harvest time. Daddy would use another type of machinery to cut these stalks up, and they will rot in the field and become fertilizer for next year's crop.

This machine was hitched to the mules, and was called a stalk cutter. It had a seat for Daddy to ride above the blades that turn to cut the stalks. Sometimes, Daddy would use a hay rake, similar to the stalk cutter, to rake the stalks into piles and burn them when the weather was right -not windy, so a fire could get out of hand. Fire was handled with lots of ease and care. The neighbors were aware when each one was intending to burn a field. They were ready and eager to help each other at a time like that.

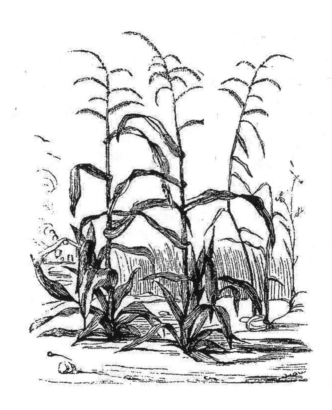

CHAPTER 18
GARDEN

Spring or fall would be the time for Daddy and Mama to start a garden. They would discuss where each type of row would be placed, for each type of vegetable to be planted. Then the work would begin. The whole garden patch had to be turned with a plow that dug deep in the ground and broke roots of things like grass and old vines and this turned up the ground and made it hard to walk on. Then he would use the harrow, a tool that had blades that went round and round. The mule pulled this type of plow too. Now he would make the rows ready for the different seed that would be planted, or that had to be set out. Some rows would need extra things done to them as the plants grew. Some would be planted with the planter that used fertilizer at the same time —as with the crops he had been planting. Some would be hand dropped in a hole dug for each kind of seed.

Early corn was planted —maybe three or four rows. We

called these "roast-n-ears." It did not grow as tall as the field corn and had a sweeter taste to it, but it grew just as the field corn.

String beans were planted with the planter and we usually had two rows of these, (as long as the garden was.) After plowing and hoeing grass from around the beans, they began to have runners. Daddy would put a number of poles between the two rows where he usually plowed, and string wire from one pole to another, stretching it tight. Then with tobacco twine, we would wrap around the bean vine. We would start the vines up the twine that had been looped over the wire and stretched to another bean vine on the other row. We did this on down the two rows of beans until all the vines were on the strings and wire. We called these string beans. They grew long and hung on the vines, easy to pick and easy to snap before cooking. They were green, and firm. We snapped both ends off when preparing to cook them. Putting the poles up and digging the holes (with the hole digger) and stringing the wires required a lot of work. Daddy used the digger a lot of times, as he needed to put up a pole in many places. Hole diggers had a part on the bottom, that was metal and strong with both pointed ends sharp, to help dig. There was one on each handle. These blades were attached to each other and were also attached to the two handles. When pushed into the ground, and the handles pulled apart at the top, it would hold the dirt it dug up. When lifted out of the hole and the handles were turned loose, the dirt would fall out, wherever he wanted to drop it. Each time it went back into the hole, the hole got deeper. When it was as deep as he wanted it, he could place the pole in the hole, and fill in the hole around the pole with the dirt that was dug out and still have dirt left over, to spread around the pole.

Runner type butter beans were done the same way as the string beans. We did not plant many running butter beans, as we liked the bunch type best. There would be four or five rows of bunch, butter beans. These could be planted with a planting plow or by hand. Someone using a hoe would dig a small amount of dirt out of the ground, leaving a shallow hole to drop the seed in, and then cover this hole back with the same dirt.

Black eyed peas, purple hull peas, small green peas (early or English peas), all were considered bunch beans, and were planted the same way peas were. There might be two rows each in our garden.

Squash seed were planted so the vines could spread in the middle of the row and, as they grew, blooms formed on these vines and then the tiny yellow squash came on the stems of the vines that were pinned down in the ground. As the squash grew, the necks of the squash curved and the bottom part of the squash became bigger.

Cucumbers were grown similar to the squash. Cucumbers were dark green and grew to be quite long, Mama gathered her cucumbers before they got so big.

Cucumbers were peeled and put in a dish with vinegar at mealtime. Sometimes Mama would slice them and put them in jars and cans, to use later. The cucumbers and squash had tiny seeds, but these are edible.

Beets are a dark red fruit and are grown from seeds. They have roots that are big and round like the turnip root. The tops of the beet have leaves and form a bush, and they are easy to pull out of the ground. Mama liked to put vinegar on these for meals also, to go with vegetables. She also canned these.

Onions are planted as bulbs, in a row, covered lightly. As they grow, the tops have shoots (straight long blades) that have blooms on them. But the onions grow into a good-sized bulb under the shoots in the ground, and these are easy to pull up. They have a skin on them that would need to be peeled off before using them for eating and cooking. The blades are good to eat when the plants are young. The roots on the bulb have to be cut off, to use in eating and cooking.

Okra seeds were planted and grew up to be a stalk, tall and straight with leaves that were prickly and made me itch. Okra has a green pod and has a stem at the top that holds it on to the stalk. The bottom has a sharp point on it. Okra has seeds in the pods and these seeds, when green, are edible and so is the outer covering of the okra. Only one row would be needed of okra.

Tomatoes were plants that Daddy bought. These were set out like the tobacco plants. Or, one could plant them using a hoe and putting the plant and fertilizer in before covering the bottom of the plant, as with the tobacco plants. These plants were fragile, and must be handled with care. The tomato plants grow into a bush and blooms and then the little green, tomatoes would come on the plants, and the leaves helped protect them. They grew bigger and started changing color. They were most delicious when picked from the vine and were firm and red. Even the ripe tomatoes had to be handled with care, as they would bruise easily.

Sometimes the tomatoes were so heavy, the stalks had to have help to hold them up. Daddy would have small stakes of wood he used to stake these with, and a string would be wrapped around the tomato stalk and limbs and onto the stake. Daddy usually planted several rows of tomatoes, as Mama canned many jars of them to use in the winter months.

Bell Peppers were green or red. We usually would have only a few hills of peppers. These were plants to set out too. When the peppers grew heavy, Daddy would stake them as he did the tomatoes. Mama had a can that she had set a pepper plant out in that grew tiny pods of pepper. With these little pods, she made pepper sauce by putting them in a bottle and pouring in vinegar and putting a cork stopper in the top to seal it. We used it with our vegetables —mostly with turnips or mustard greens.

Irish potatoes were the most common, potatoes planted

in our area. This is the white potato, used in so many ways —boiled, fried, mashed, creamed, and used in soups and salads. These potatoes had spots on them we called eyes. We would cut the potato eyes off of the potato and plant the eyes. They came up in a bunch-type bush. The potatoes grew under the bush and had to be dug, from under it. We used a spoon to dig the potatoes that we used for cooking. And we saved potatoes at the end of the season, to plant next year.

Sweet potatoes grew like the watermelon and squash, with long vines that pinned down in the rows around them. These were set out in slips. Daddy had a special place he built for bedding potatoes. He dug a ditch about waist deep and we put the potatoes that he had saved in this hole and covered them up and made a mound of dirt over them. When the time came to plant, he would plant these potatoes and the slips would be cut off and reset in the garden. Usually two rows of sweet potatoes were enough for us.

Sweet potatoes were a light color of red, and Mama made the best sweet potato pies. They could be baked in the oven and eaten with butter or with meat. Mama would make candied yams, cooking them with sugar, butter and cinnamon. Good! Both of these potatoes, Irish and sweet, have a different taste to them and both are good.

Greens are a leafy-type of vegetable that are different colors of green. Turnips have roots and the leaves are wide and long and are good with or without the roots cooked with them. They do not need to be cooked long. With cornbread and ham hocks (cooked in the same pot), even the broth cooked out of them is good.

Mustard greens do not have roots as the turnips do. Mustard leaves are larger, and some leaves are crinkled and some are straight. Cooked as the turnips —with a piece of meat and a little lard and maybe a dash of sugar. And they are good served with pepper sauce too (not to hot!)

Collard greens are similar to mustard, except that their leaves are a much different color of green and the leaves are much broader. Like all the greens, they require lots of washing, cleaning and cutting before cooking with lard and meat to be good!

There was always work to be done in the garden. As plants came up so did the weeds and the grass, and these had to be hoed. The plants had to be plowed, fertilized, and hoed before gathering either for a meal or for canning. Butter beans and peas had to be shelled and washed, and snap beans had to have the ends broken off and the beans broken in several pieces.

Jars had to be found and washed and lids had to be found to fit each jar. These were boiled in a pan of water and turned over to dry on a towel, ready to be filled. Daddy would be needed to tighten each jar lid; to be sure it would hold its seal tightly. Before we had a pressure cooker, we put the jars in the wash pot and boiled them after they were filled. When Mama said they were ready to be taken out of the pot, they were turned on the lid side to cool. Then they were checked to see if the lids were still tight, and put on the shelves in the smokehouse. Everything— required work every day. All the items in the garden were planted in their proper season year around!

CHAPTER 19
MELONS

Watermelons and cantaloupes were usually planted only for our own food, and might be planted in the garden or on the end of corn rows. It takes lots of space for watermelon and cantaloupes to grow. Daddy prepared the land for these as with many of the vegetables. He prepared in a row that had a hill, in the center of the row. He would use a hoe a to dig a small hole and one of us would drop the seeds in this hole, and he would cover the hole back with the soil he has dug out with the hoe, as we planted the watermelon or cantaloupe seed. The rows would need to be wide apart, to allow the vines to spread. The vines would have pins that attached to the earth and held the vines in place. There would be blooms on the vines and these blooms would become small melons or cantaloupes. Watermelons come in several different varieties. Daddy especially liked the dark green ones. Sometimes he would get seeds from someone that grew the stripped melons too and plant them. The inside of a melon is red, with black seeds. In the middle of the melon and around the inside of the rind, there is a ring of white, which no one eats. It protects the red part of the melon, or so we thought. The white part is tough and the red part is soft and juicy. Good, with a sprinkle of salt. Daddy would thump on a watermelon, to tell by the sound of the thump if it was ripe. He usually was right every time!

Cantaloupes are small and very near round, and there are markings as if to show where you are to slice them. Daddy went by the color of the stems the cantaloupes grew on from their vines, to tell if they were ripe. Cantaloupes have a little bit of tough white rind under the rough and tough outer layer. The inside of the cantaloupe is a light pink in color, and there are a number of seeds that grow onto the meat, which is soft, but firm inside and there is a empty spot in the middle so the seed are easy to scrape out, when cut open. Slices were handed around to each other at picnics and at snack times, and a little salt and pepper is very delicious with the slices. They are eaten by biting into the slices. The slices of both watermelons and cantaloupes were then given to the hogs. The watermelon rinds were very good to use to wash ones hands in —to get the gunk of tobacco off from ones hands.

Many watermelon seeds were used in a spitting contest. Some of the games played at gatherings were to see who could spit the seed the farthest, or who could get the most seed in a jar or a can from a certain distance. All in fun!

Remembering back, we had to hoe the grass and weeds from these watermelons and cantaloupes and, as their vines got in the way for Daddy to plow the last time, we would turn these vines out of the way of the plow. Always one more job to do!

Seeds from both the watermelon and cantaloupes were saved and dried to use to plant next year.

We could always count on "company coming" at this season of the year. Mama's folks from North Georgia liked to come this time of the year to be in on the fresh vegetables and the melons.

CHAPTER 20
FRUIT TREES

It seemed we were always getting small trees to plant from different places, wherever we went. Peaches, pears, figs and plums, all were so delicious, and it takes so long for these to start producing; years, sometimes. These trees had a special place to be planted and Daddy fertilized and watered them faithfully. I can never remember not having peach and pear trees in this area, next to the house on the south side. There were never more than two or three peach trees and mostly only one pear tree. There were always enough fruit from these trees for Mama to use to make pies and to preserve and to make jellies. Many were shared with those that did not have these trees. The fruit from both trees always fell to the ground, making a mess to be cleaned up. We would gather the peaches and wash them and let them dry. Then, using a very sharp knife, we would peel the protective skin from the peaches. We would slice the peaches and get the rather large seeds from the center and enjoy them as they were, or fix them the way Mama wanted to use them. If she was going to cook them to preserve them, we hunted the glass pint fruit jars and washed them and she steamed them in a pan of very hot water on the top of her stove.

Mama made sure they were very clean before filling them and putting the lids on tightly. Daddy would see if they were tight and if not, he was strong and would make sure they were tight.

Pears were handled in the same manner, except that than they do not have a large seed in the center. The

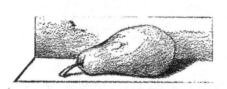 core of the pear was hard and would need to be cored out, with a special tool. Most of the ones she did not make into preserves were cut in halves

and special sugar syrup, made with the juice of the pears and sugar cooked together, was poured into the pint jars and sealed for later use.

CHAPTER 21
BEES

The fruit that fell from the fruit trees was a welcome sight for the bees. The bees loved this, especially the honeybees and, while the fruit was on the ground, everyone had to be careful or they could be stung. Daddy liked the honeybees. He would build little houses for them. We called these houses "bee hives." And the bees knew they were welcome to live there. Many would seem to come back every year. (?) How can one tell one Bee from another? Daddy seemed to know when to expect the bees to come and had their hives ready.

He had special clothes he wore when working around the bees. He had to be covered well. He had a hat that had a facemask that he could lift up when he wanted to. His sleeves had to be long and tied around the wrists. His pants legs had to be tied too, and he always wore the high top shoes,. The bees had to be kept off of his skin completely. Without the bees, none of the vegetables or crops that had blooms would make at all. Fruit trees and flowers, all have to be pollinated by bees. So strange they work on all plants and yet the variety never mixes. The Lord created each little bee to do what it was created to do. Yes, the bees would get to one's skin and would sting and it does hurt! Daddy had a smoker a tool that he used when checking the hives to see when the trays inside were packed with honey. He would spray a little smoke into a hive and the bees would go out, but not very far. If the hives were pretty full, he would take the trays to the house where he and Mama would melt the honey out of the trays and clean the trays before replacing them in the hives. Mama and Daddy knew how to harvest the honey, and we all enjoyed the honey with our butter and biscuits.

CHAPTER 22
BLACKBERRIES

Blackberries were one of our favorites. They were mostly wild, not cultivated, and grew by the side of the road or in ditches. Mama would go with us to pick a bucket of blackberries. When picking blackberries, we were always on the lookout for snakes, or a plant that could be poisonous, and would make one break out in a rash that could require going to a Doctor. Blackberries have lots of sticker briars on their stalks and a prick of these hurts! So, we had to be very careful when picking blackberries.

Mama made the best blackberry pies! They almost made having to get the briars picked from fingers,

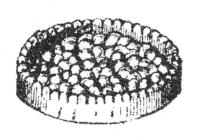

worth it! Blackberries crushed and strained to make blackberry juice were so good!

CHAPTER 23
SCUPPERNONGS

Scuppernongs are set out as small plants. Some say you have to have a male and female plant to expect to harvest any scuppernongs. There are different varieties. Ours were purple, some are green, but when they are ripe — oh so good! The juice is so sweet and the meat inside is good, but the seeds need to be spit out. The skins of the, scuppernongs are not edible either. When Daddy planted the scuppernongs, he watched them and decided when he needed to build a frame for them. He puts four posts in an area and one post in the center of these, where the plant was. Then, he would attach a wire or a string around the vines as they grew, and attach these to the frame he had built for them. This frame held the heavy vines off the ground and made the gathering of them — if only a hand full at a time— easier.

After the season for them was over, they would lose their leaves and the vines would be strong and tough. Daddy would cut them back, and year after year they would continue to bear fruit. He would fertilize and water them. Our scuppernongs vine was near the other fruit trees, on the south side of the house, handy for a snack.

CHAPTER 24
CANE / SYRUP

Sugar cane grows tall and slender stalks, jointed about every three inches with a tassel at the top, just as corn does. There are different varieties of cane. Ours had peelings that were mostly purple, but some were green. This peeling, or covering, was tough and strong to protect the cane. The stalk had roots that went deep into the ground, and this helped hold the cane stalk up to grow tall and straight. In the fall of the year, at the time of harvesting the cane, some of the stalks were put in a mound of dirt. They were then covered with straw and another layer of dirt to protect them.

In the spring at planting time, they would be dug up and Daddy would make furrows in the rows and lay the stalks in the furrows, covering them lightly. They would sprout from the joints, and the plants that would grow from these would have strong stalks.

Harvesting the cane was never easy. Daddy used a tool we called a stripper. This tool had pieces of thin metal on the lower end of the handle to strip off the leafy part of the stalk.

He would take the cane to the mill, where a machine, powered by a mule, would grind the cane. The cane would be fed into the proper place and the juice would be caught in a tub or containers. The stalks were squeezed to get the juice from them and were then piled in a place to be burned later. The roots and tassels had been trimmed off before hauling them to the cane mill. It was a treat to go to the cane patch and cut down a stalk of cane, peel it, and cut it into joints. The round pieces would be cut to fit into our mouth to chew. We would get the sweet juice and swallow it.

The juice was brought home and an appointed time was made to fit the Syrup Maker's schedule. He did most of the syrup making in our community and had the big vat that the juice was put in to cook the juice until it became thick and was syrup. Daddy would take the mule and wagon and go wherever the "vat" was used last and haul it to our house. Wood had been cut and was ready to start heating this vat of juice, as directed by this neighbor who made syrup. It takes a long time to cook the water from the juice and, even though the vat may have been near full at the start, when it ended up as syrup in the bottom of the vat, it was not very deep. The syrup had to cool some before it could be bottled, and a cork stopper would be put in the top of the bottle to preserve the syrup. As a rule, we never ran out of syrup from one year to the next harvesting time. We ate syrup with most of our meals. The syrup was stored in the smokehouse on shelves that Daddy had prepared for them and the canned goods Mama made each year.

CHAPTER 25
SOAP MAKING

Mama always saved her used cooking grease. She used lard, rendered from meats at hog killing time, for all her cooking and never threw any away. She saved it in jars and pans, and she would buy many cans of potash and have ready to use when she had time to make her home made soap. She would instruct us on how to fix the big black wash pot, getting the wood ready to put the fire around the pot. Then, she would put the grease and the potash in the pot, stir this and tell us how much water to bring her. She would stir this many more times. We would keep the fire going around the wash pot, and when the water had cooked out of the grease and potash, there would be a tallow like substance in the bottom of it. Mama would prepare a table with cloths on it and take the soap out of the wash pot, flattening out the mounds of soap to a thickness she wanted. Then with a big kitchen knife, she would cut the soap into small mounds and wrap this in wax paper. This would be put in boxes, ready to be used when needed. The soap was used for many purposes. It really did clean the dirt out of the work clothes and greasy fingers from working with farm tools. We had this soap to use at the wash pan on the side porch. On a shelf Daddy made for a water bucket, there was a gourd dipper and a small bowl to hold the soap. This was our clean-up spot before eating meals.

Sometimes, when we had the money, Mama might buy a bar of Oxygen soap or a bar of Ivory soap from the store. But these were rare purchases.

Our towels were usually made of sacks that flour came in, that Mama would hem. We used them every day. When we had company coming, we used our better towels and soap.

CHAPTER 26
WASH DAY

Monday was usually a big day for washing clothes, weather permitting, after other regular chores were finished. Water was drawn and toted to tubs. Clothes were gathered and taken outside to the tubs that had been filled with water, and these clothes had to be sorted (color-wise). Next the wash pot had to be filled, as directed by Mama, as much as she wanted in the pot. A fire was started with papers, cobs, trash and wood to start the water boiling. Mama used the rub board on the clothes in soapy water and then put the clothes in the wash pot to boil. After this, she would take them out of the pot using the battling stick to gather the clothes on. She would lift them into a tub to rinse the soapy water out. The clothes were then put into another tub to rinse again, before as much of the water as possible could be squeezed and wrung out of them. Then these clothes were placed in a pan to take to the clothesline. Daddy had put up the tall poles for the clothesline using the hole digger to dig a hole and hold the poles up. He would then string a heavy wire between the poles to hang the clothes on to dry in the sunshine and wind. If the clothes were big and heavy, the line would sag. Another pole or board would be needed to prop up the line, by putting the end of the pole under the wire and pushing it up. This would make the line stay higher and the end of the pole or board would press in the ground, leaning to anchor it. Clothes smelled so clean and fresh after being dried in the fresh air and sunshine.

Later in the week, weather permitting, Mama would say early in the morning, "Time to wash the bed sheets and towels." We went through the same routine of getting the tubs and water and the wash pot and a fire going around the wash pot, as we did with the clothes. Mama and I would strip the beds, and Daddy and the boys would haul the mattresses out to a place prepared for them on saw horses, to hold them off the ground and let them get the sunshine for the day. A saw horse looks like 'A=A. ' It had a board across two sets of these, to hold the mattress up off the ground while they aired out in the sun. (Oh how good to sleep on a clean fresh bed!)

Sometimes there would be as many as four different pots of clothes to wash and do the same way with each load. It was a full day's work with time out to cook dinner and do the dishes. The bedding was so large and heavy that sometimes Daddy would have to help Mama squeeze and wring them out and hang them on the clotheslines. It was for sure the extra pole or board would be used, to keep the sheets from touching the ground. The sheets were hung over the clothesline, but still needed to be held with the clothes pins to keep them on the clothes wire.

Mama had made a sack with a belt around the top to slip over our head to carry the clothespins, so we could get to them easily, as we needed to pin the clothes on the line. Then came the time to bring the washed clothes in the house to fold and put away. Clothes that needed to be ironed were put in a basket to starch later and to hang out to dry again, before sprinkling them and rolling them to let the dampness soak in. If wash day for the bedding had been near the end of the week, we would take the wash water from the pot and first tub to scrub the floors, while the beds were out sunning.

CHAPTER 27
SCRUBBING / MOPPING

Mama made her scrub mop. Daddy had made a board about a foot and half long, one foot wide, and one and a half inches thick. He made holes in it and the holes had to be big enough so she could push corn shucks through. She soaked them in hot water, to shrink them enough to push and pull them through these holes. Then with an ax or a real sharp knife, she would trim the bottoms of the shucks to about two inches from the board, and this made the scrub mop stiff for scrubbing. The mop was pushed along by the long handle that was placed in the middle of the board of the mop. We toted the water by the bucket full, for Mama to use for scrubbing the floors and then for the rinsing. We took the rinse water from the tubs and used clean fresh

water, drawn up from the well for the last rinsing.

After this hard work, we might get a rest time, with maybe a glass of buttermilk and some gingerbread?

CHAPTER 28
STRAW BROOMS

Thinking about brooms, Mama would let us go with her along the edge of the woods or down the county road to find straw to make hers. She would cut off the straw from these bushes and bring them home. She would take a cotton sheet to spread on the ground. She would strip the extra leaves and things off the straws, trim the tops a little and get some twine and wrap the lower parts in a hand full. Bingo, she had a good broom to sweep the floor with. We did carry lots of grit in the house on our bare feet. She was always sweeping the floors.

When it was time to bring in the mattresses, and pillows, Daddy and the boys did this. They were careful not to track up Mama's clean floors. We got the sheets off the lines and made the beds. Then we brought in the towels and anything else that Mama had washed, like scarves or tablecloths. These were folded put back in their proper places. Chore time again, before supper!

CHAPTER 29
GOURDS

Gourd seeds were planted around the edge of the yard or around the edge of the garden. Gourds were used in many ways at our house. The reason we wanted lots of gourds, was to make nests for the birds migrating to our place every year.

The martins are small birds and need no help from anyone but they appreciated the gourd's nesting place that Daddy provided. Each year Daddy would see to it that the gourds were in good shape and replaced the ones that needed to be replaced. The gourd is similar to the squash, and melon families. Gourds have vines and blooms and would pin down the running vines that covered the area they were in. The little gourds looked like squash, with their slender necks and fat middles. Squash turn yellow, but gourds turn tan, or light brown. Gourds grow much bigger than squash. When they grew as big as Daddy wanted them, he would pick them from the vines. He had a special place to put them in, a sunny spot to dry. Later Daddy would cut round holes in the sides of the gourds and bore a hole in the necks of them. He would attach a wire to this part of the gourd, to hang on the tall post. He had worked on the post, to get crosspieces at the top of the pole to hold the gourds that the martins would build their nests in. There were many ways Daddy used the gourds. He made soap dishes. He would put little screws and nails in and hang them in convenient places, to keep things separated. When the gourds got dry, the seeds inside were loose, and as we shook the gourds, we pretended to make music with them.

CHAPTER 30
MARTINS

The martins were guards for our baby chickens. The hawks liked to fly into the yard and catch a little baby chicken or a young chicken in its beak and fly away with it. Martins would gang up on them or anything that bothered these little chickens, and they would scream and fight with their wings and beaks, until they would leave the chicken alone.

It might even be one of our house pets, the dog or cat that would go after the chickens. The martins knew when to attack. We did not have to feed or water or take care of them in any way. They were a joy to watch, as they seemed so happy.

CHAPTER 31
CHICKENS

Roosters are the males of the chicken species. The crowing one, "the ruler," of the roost. Hens, the female of the chicken species, lay the eggs, sit on the nest until the chicks are hatched, and then tend to their welfare until they are old enough to fend for themselves. Pullets are hens that are too young to lay eggs (teenagers). All of the species except the baby chicks (biddies) are edible. And most are raised for the purpose of becoming food for the table. Eggs are only laid by the hens, but all eggs do not hatch. The male and female of the species must mate for the eggs to hatch, and the little biddies hatch from fertile eggs only. All the eggs are edible.

Everyone had a choice of the breed of chickens they wanted to raise for their family. Our family liked the Rhode Island Red breed the best. This breed had red feathers, and we came to know that this was the best kind for us to raise. They also had the best meat for eating.

Daddy built a chicken house for them. Inside, were poles spaced like steps, from the bottom to the top, and the number of the poles depended on how many steps Daddy planned to make. These poles would be where the chickens could roost and, hopefully, no wild animal would come after them. Many chickens would go missing, and we would find that something had gotten them, killed them and dragged them away. The chickens would stay at night in the pens. In the day time, they would be busy hunting —scratching in most any place to find some bug or worm to eat. At night we would try and remember to close the hen house door. Another chore to remember!

There were many places Daddy had built up, off the ground, for the hens to lay their eggs in nests they made. Some of the hens refused to lay in there nest there, and they hid their nest from us. These, we would soon find, and gather the eggs from their nests, the same as the other nests.

Late in the afternoon was the best time to gather the eggs to carry into the house. The eggs Mama did not use in her cooking were kept in a box ready to take with the cream and butter to the store to sell on Saturday.

Mama had a special place where she put the eggs that she knew were needed for hatching and were fertile, and she kept these separate from the ones we ate. When a hen began to stay longer on a nest, Mama would begin to get these eggs ready to put in the nest with this hen. She would take a pencil and mark round and round on these eggs, and then put them under the hen in the nest. This hen would only leave the nest to get food and water. She would come right back and sit on the nest to keep the eggs warm until time for them to hatch little biddies.

Sometimes, another hen would sneak on the nest while she was off to get food and water and lay an egg. When the "setting" hen came back, she would make the new hen leave. Mama would check the nests every day and gather the eggs not marked.

We would listen to hear if the hen started clucking, or if we saw eggshells on the ground near the nests. Sometimes we could even see a baby chick pecking its way out of the shell. The hen would help it by pecking at the shell and throwing the shell out of the nest. Then it was time to build a small pen for the hen and her brood of baby chicks. Sometimes this was an old washtub, turned over with a stick under it, to hold it up for them to be protected from our cats and dog and from other animals and large birds, like hawks. Daddy said we could use the tobacco sticks if we wanted too. This was fun to build, and we could watch the little chicks scamper around and hear the hen scolding them, clucking to them when she had something to share with them. They would always hurry to her. Daddy had prepared for the food to feed them. The last time he went to the mill to have corn ground for our meal, he also had some corn cracked fine for the chickens. Their water was in a quart jar, with a saucer-like lid on it. When the jar was turned upside down, water ran down into the saucer. The saucer stayed full of water as long as there was water in the quart jar. The feed trough had small holes in it, so they had to stick their heads in these small holes to peck at the cracked corn. Otherwise, they would soon have it on the ground, scratching for it.

The hens had a hard time keeping up with the little chicks. As the chicks grew bigger, she would soon give up and start back laying eggs again, leaving the small chicks for us to look after. The chicken coops would be put away, waiting for the next batch of baby chickens to hatch.

The martins came every year and made their nests in the gourds Daddy fixed for them. They were lots of help in keeping the hawks and things from catching the small biddies. When they were around, we enjoyed watching them as they protected things around our house.

Any day now, Mama would suggest it would soon be time to have fresh fried chicken for dinner. When she said this, we were anxious to see who would be the one to get to wring the chicken's neck. First, the chicken Mama picked out had to be caught. She would give us a cold biscuit and tell us to tear it up and drop the pieces by our feet and call," chic, chic, chic," over and over until they came. Then we would bend down or stoop over and grab that chicken. Then, we would put our hand around its neck and flip the chicken around and around until its neck was broken, and then lay it down on the ground until it quit kicking before taking it in the house to Mama.

Mama had her own way of dressing the chicken. She had hot water ready to dip the chicken in before picking the feathers off. When the feathers were all off, she had a piece of paper and a match and would set the paper on fire and hold the chicken over the fire. This was to swing off the tiny hair-like feathers called pin feathers. There were many ways to cut the chicken. The idea was to get enough pieces so everyone could get more than one serving. A hard day's work made everyone hungry, especially for fried chicken.

Mama's way was to have two wings, two thighs, two legs, and two legs with the feet attached (but with the toenails cut off). There was not much meat on these, but they were good to gnaw on.

The pulley bone, which we all wanted to see, (when we pulled it apart) said who would get married first. The breast could be cut in two so it would make one more serving. Then we had two sides, —bony but good — one backbone, one neck, one gizzard and one liver. Sometimes, Mama would take the bony pieces of chicken and boil them and make dumplings to drop in the broth these cooked in. Very good!

She would salt and pepper the frying pieces and roll them around in flour until they were coated well, and then drop these in a frying pan of hot lard until they were brown and done.

After taking the chicken up out of the hot lard, she would sprinkle flour in the lard and let it brown, adding some salt and pepper to this and pouring lots of milk into the mix. She let this gravy cook until done. Ummmm Good!

The Irish potatoes had to be peeled with a spoon before they were put in a pot to boil. When, the potatoes were ready to mash, Mama would let me use the pint jar to mash these potatoes until there were no lumps. She would add milk and butter and beat them together with a table fork and they were put in a bowl, ready to go on the table. With the pan of Mama's biscuits to go with that good thick milk gravy and the creamed potatoes and fried chicken, and Daddy saying a blessing and thanking God for such a wonderful meal, we were happy and very full, in a very few minutes.

The jolly rooster strutted around before the hens and the pullets, bragging about the way he looked. He was always crowing and primping, to let them know how good he felt about his good looks, or sometimes fighting off any other roosters that came near his "flock." And then he would have one more loud crowing session, just to remind everyone he would be crowing in the morning, to wake everyone up.

As the roosters and hens got older, it would be time for Mama to have one of these in a pen for a day or two, before killing one of them. They would be dressed as the fryers were before, and were either baked or boiled for a meal. Mama would make cornbread, mixed with eggs, onions and sage, together with milk and broth (that the chicken was cooked in,). Mama stirred all this together with pieces of meat added, and made this to be chicken dressing. Then this mixture baked until Mama said it was just right, and we had another wonderful meal.

Some of the chicken would be placed on a platter to be eaten, and some were made into a salad with pickles and onions added and other things, as Mama desired.

CHAPTER 32
HOGS

Hogs on Daddy's farm, were there, for two reasons. One was to be used for meat for the family and the other was for the money that was received when he sold them. Hogs, nor their pigs, were pets. We never gave them names.

Hogs are Swine. Males are boars and females are sows, and the baby hogs are pigs. Swine can be several colors and special breeds. Ours were black and the pigs —when first born —were pink and their skin at birth was soft but, as they grew, the skin became tough and had wiry hair as did the large hogs. The hogs had a special pen to be kept in, and we had to draw the water and tote it by the bucket to their trough, keeping it filled as often as we could. They were messy, and would turn the trough over to get to wallow in the mud.

Daddy bought special food we called mash for them. This was mixed with milk, and helped make them fat. We also shucked the corn for them, and Daddy had some corn cracked for them too. Hogs were fed, like the mules and cows, twice a day. We might need to tote more water to them. It was fun to watch them play in the mud, and they liked to wallow in it. Sows with pigs were put in separate pens, to protect the pigs —as boars were known to eat them if they could get to them.

The best time to have a hog killing was in the winter months. This was because there would be fewer flies that would go after the fresh smell of the meat, and also because the farmers had more time to allow for this work. Hog killing took lots of planning and was lots of work. A lot of things had to be prepared for.

First thing, the ones to be killed were separated from the rest of the herd and put in smaller pens, so they did not have room to roam around and walk off fat that we hoped to put on them. The more weight put on them, the more lard would be made to use in our cooking. A place to hang the hog after it was killed had to be built. It would be two posts; holes dug deep enough (with the hole diggers) to be sure the poles would not bend. Dirt packed around the poles to hold them in place. The top pole would need to be bolted down to each of the poles; far enough apart to put the hooks, (which were used to hold the hog's feet,) and to allow the men room to work around the hanging hog. The hog would be hung with its head down, and split from its tail area to its neck and allowed to bleed. The blood was caught in a tub, to be buried in a hole, (dug away from the house). Tubs to be used to catch the entrails of the hog, for the women to clean and prepare, were needed to be ready. A vat was needed, big enough to hold lots of water to be heated to take the hair off the hog after it was killed. Not everyone had a vat big enough for this, but a neighbor did who allowed everyone to use it. It took

 several men to load and unload it from the wagon. The mules had a load to pull the vat, made of iron. The top of the vat was open and slanted from the bottom center up and out to the top. It was about five feet wide at the top. The vat held lots of water, to be drawn and carried by the bucket to the vat, before the fire was built under it to heat the water. Wood had to be ready to use around the vat, and this was stacked near the area for the vat to be placed.

A table had to be built, to place the hog on to scrape the wiry hair off, and allow the men to cut the meat up in pieces to handle. Daddy would need two sawhorses (A==A) to hold a large sheet of wood or boards to form the tabletop, with a space to work with saws and sharp knives, an ax and a hammer to use, if needed. These would be put in the vat to scald before using. This table would be scrubbed with soapy hot water before time to put the hog on it to scrape it. It would be scrubbed again after the scraping, to be sure no hair or anything was left on the table that could contaminate the meat.

A smaller table would be needed for the women, to use for their working space, like the larger one, a little away from where the men would be working. There would be lots of towels or cloths used, so Mama might tear up an old sheet to have enough clean cloths, to be used and ready for this day.

A date to do this had to be planned. Help needed to work with Daddy and Mama. One neighbor would tell another, and soon the word would get around. Then people would come by and volunteer to help. They knew, when their time came, others would do the same for them. When the day came, all was in place —wood for the fire to use around the vat, a place to hang the hog, ready with the hooks in place on the top pole. Tables were ready, with needed tools in place and tubs were handy. Now, to get the hog killed and continue from there. Sometime Daddy would shoot the hog in the head, or use a large hammer or mallet to knock it in the head. The neighbors would help Daddy get the hog to the vat and help roll it around in the hot water and lift it out to the table to scrape the wiry hair off. After scrapping the hair off, they would lift the hog and hang it on the scaffold by its hind feet, then pour hot water over the body of the hog to rinse anything that could contaminate it before continuing with their work.

The head would be at the bottom of the scaffold, and Daddy or one of the men would split the hog, from its tail to its head. A tub was placed under the hog and would catch the entrails —heart, liver— and, separated from the hog they were carried to the women's table.

The tools the men used had been scalded in the vat and placed in a covered container, ready to be used when needed. The feet were trimmed, of the nails on all, four feet. The feet were cut off from the legs and placed in a pan for the women to take care of. The head and the tail would be cut off and given to the women to work with.

Next came the job of dividing the body of the hog; a job for the men. It would take more than one man to handle the carcass of the hog and hold while others would saw or cut or use the ax to cut off the parts, as these were held together with tendons that were strong and not easy to cut apart. Hams, shoulders, sides and backbone (after being cut in smaller pieces) were given to the women to finish dressing. The hams, sides, and shoulders were fixed to hang, on a hook in the smokehouse to smoke (cure.)

When this was finished, the men scalded the area they had been working on, and took apart the table used by them, along with the scaffold. Daddy had these put in a special place, to be used again next time. The vat had to be cleaned and loaded on the wagon with the mules ready to hitch up to return the vat to the neighbor that it belonged to.

Mama and the women, whose husbands had helped Daddy, were still working with the head and other parts of the hog. Mama had started a dinner at breakfast time and slipped away to go in the house to prepare it, for they would all be eating dinner. A "*Company's Coming*" dinner would be served. I would set the table and peel and slice the onions, and then go to the smokehouse to get peaches and tomatoes and pickles to go with the peas and butter beans. While I did this, Mama fried some fresh liver she had just sliced and peppered, and rolled in flour. A brown thick broth in the bottom of the frying pan was used to make thick onion gravy to go with the fried liver. Sweet tea was ready to pour when she had time to chip the ice for it. Potatoes were creamed, and corn bread and biscuits were fresh from the oven.

The women covered the things they were working with tightly, to keep anything from getting to this while they ate dinner. My little brother chose to guard the area and call out if things came around it. He had a stick he pretended was a gun, and was pleased to be, "guarding."

After the dinner, the men went out to the wagon and rested while the ladies went back to their work. Mama and I did the dishes and then we joined them. The hog's head was split open and the brains were taken out of the head and I was allowed to wash these in a pan of cold water. The brains were in a bloody substance and, in the water, this would tear off very easily. I washed these through other waters and put them in a dish and put it in the icebox. We would have these for breakfast with eggs.

The entrails were to be washed many times, to be sure they were clean. Some of these (I was showed how to do) were scraped, to get the inside thickness out, by using the back of a table knife or a spoon. These were used to stuff ground meat that had been seasoned for sausage and hung in the smokehouse to be smoked (cured). Some of the sausage was saved to fry in patties. We loved either kind, with syrup and biscuits, any time!

Chitterlings were one of our favorites when they were cooked right. They had been washed several times, and then Mama boiled them until she said they were done. She would season them as she did her other foods, adding some lard and a dash of sugar, and cook this for a short time, and then serve them. Sometimes she would batter and fry them. The day of hog killing was a busy day and everyone was very tired and ready to go home and, of course, everyone had chores to do before getting to bed to rest!

CHAPTER 33
MULES

Mules were our workers, hitched to a plow to cultivate, plant, or haul, anything, they were always used to help with things and do as they were told to. Our mules, named Ada and Minnie, knew their names, and we knew they did. They were very strong and obeyed directions given to them. "Whoa," "Back up," "Get up," were some of the words they understood. They knew to be still when being harnessed to work. They had a pen, built with a high fence, to keep them from jumping over to run away. They loved to nip at each other, and they were frisky and bucked when they played with each other. It was fun to watch, but we never went very close to them at this time.

If they got out of the pen, they were

hard to round up and catch. They loved to be free. They were not allowed in the fields (when the crops were gathered,) as they might hurt the other animals. The stalls, where they were fed and watered, had straw on the ground. The stalls had to be cleaned. The men had to do the cleaning. Mules did not like women and would kick or bite them.

CHAPTER 34
CHURCH

The church was just maybe a mile up the road from us, and sometimes we children would walk to meet our neighbors and walk together to the church. Mama and Daddy rode in the truck. Sunday school was held in the mornings and preaching was held once a month (after Sunday School.) On Sunday night we had B.Y.P.U, another form of bible study. In this, we would have a contest and compete with each group, learning names of the books in the bible and other things the adult teachers taught us.

One of our neighbors had a model 'T' vehicle. She rode by our house every Sunday going to church, to teach Sunday school. It was fun to see her go by. She sat so straight and held onto the steering wheel real tight, always looking straight ahead. Our folks would never suggest that she might give us a ride, and we never asked.

Daddy was an ordained deacon of the church, and sometimes he would lead singing. One of his favorite songs was "Trust and Obey." The Church had a piano and several of the ladies could play. Some had organs at home, and when the community had family prayer meetings in these homes, it was so good to hear these instruments played. The church had benches to sit on and most of the mother would take a quilt to church with them, to let their young children lay on and go to sleep. The preacher always had so much to preach about, young children would get tired of being still and would easily fall asleep during the sermon.

These preachers preached, "Hell and brimstone" sermons. Some of the older men would fall asleep and someone would punch them when they snored. The preacher ignored them, and continued with his message.

In the spring on the first Sunday of the month, an all day meeting was held. Members went to the church that week and scrubbed it well and cleaned and swept the yards. A table was set up from the church almost to the graveyard, which was between the "hard shell Primitive" and the "Missionary" Baptist church. A well was already in the area, as a school used to be near the church, and was taken care of by both churches.

Members of both churches, if they chose too, were welcome to come and take part in this fellowship and dinner. Before dinner, preachers that had been invited to come and speak, would preach, one and then another, until time to eat. The members and their families brought boxes of food and hoped there would be food enough to feed the crowd expected to come. Every woman had a special thing she had cooked or baked and was eager to see and get the recipe from others of what they brought for the meal. Children were running errands and helping get things to the tables, until their mothers would tell them to go play with their friends. This is just what they wanted to hear.

Some called this, "Dinner on the ground" but it was served on tables. Each woman would spread a cloth on her portion of the tables and spread everything she had cooked and brought to share on this cloth. The host preacher got everyone's attention. He said the blessing on the food and the ones who prepared it and those visiting who shared the food. Then, he said whatever else he wanted to say to God in his prayer, and everyone said "A-MEN" after this. Plates brought from home were handed out, to be filled by everyone going to all the tables and filling their plates. Tea was ready, with glasses brought from home to let other visitors use as needed. Soon, many were sitting on the ground, with filled plates, eating and visiting with those around them. Mothers were helping the young ones fill their plates and finding them places to sit on the ground to eat.

About an hour later, people begin to go back into the church and find spaces to sit, hopefully as near a window as possible, as it had become very warm and the windows would be raised to let a breeze in. Hand fans were handed out, and they were waving back and forth to make a breeze.

As the music began, one man would sing a solo, and then a woman, then a trio or a quartet. There was foot stamping and hand clapping after each song was sung and many requests called out for, "more." Everyone was having a great time. Song leaders and singers, were giving out of breath and getting tired, so the host preacher would make the announcement, one more song, and say, "That's It Folks!" Then we would load up and go home to do our chores. There would be no service that night.

Revival time came, and the meeting would be at the church. We would sometimes have a visiting preacher. If someone joined the church, the baptismal services would be held in the "Levi Creek." This creek was a small stream of water that nature had formed. It was not very deep and the community used it as a place to go swimming at times with family, and sometimes we went fishing there. The person to be baptized would bring extra clothes (as would the Preacher.) The preacher had already asked the main questions, "Do you believe in the Lord and do you know he died for your sins? Are you ready to be submerged in this water to let the world know, you do believe, in our Lord and Savior?" This person will answer, "Yes! Then the preacher would put one of his hands over the eyes, nose and mouth of this person and put the other hand at the person's back and bend them backwards and say, " I Baptize You, (call their name), in the name of the Lord Jesus Christ, Our Savior! Amen!" He would lift the person from the water and a song was sung by the ones viewing the service, while the preacher and the one to baptized got out of the water and went to a tent made for them to get dressed in. There was a close fellowship among a community of neighbors doing the will of God. Yes "company's coming" again when Jesus comes!

CHAPTER 35
SCHOOL

The school was a big building with a high ceiling. It was between the two churches on a sandy piece of land. A well had been dug near the school, and there was an outhouse. Two women were the teachers. One taught the little children, and the other taught the larger children.

We walked to school, and everyone took a lunch, sometimes a biscuit and syrup and maybe a cookie, if Mama had time to fix cookies. There were not many students, as many had to work too much to go to school.

The most interesting part of going to school was the blackboard. We got to use the chalk and the eraser. We were glad when we were called on to go to the blackboard.

We learned to sit down and be quiet first. The teacher was very firm, and we were afraid of the teacher. If we did not mind her, she had a switch — a short piece of a tall gallberry bush, trimmed —and we knew she would use it! We also knew that when we got home, we would get another whipping from Daddy with his razor strap.

Recess was a time to play. The teachers would ring a bell

when it was time to go back in the classroom. Teachers stayed outside with us while we were playing and taught us new games, and would also hold one end of the rope for us to play jump rope. London Bridge, Hopscotch, Dodge Ball, and Drop the Handkerchief, were a few of the games we played.

The younger children did not have books to carry home to study. The older children were able to take the books home to study at home, but only if they could afford to pay for the books. Teachers used what they had to work with. They were paid a salary.

If someone in the community died, the school would close. The teachers would take us to the church for the funeral service. The only spanking I got at school was when I said that "the dead person was pretty." I did not know this was wrong.

Sometimes the well would go dry and the parents of the children in school would bring tubs of water to school until the well would be cleaned out and fresh water flowed into it again. We had to bring our own drinking cups from home to use. My cup was a little tin measuring cup. The teacher wrote my name on it.

The well was dug before a building was built because water was necessary to start any building. When a well was not furnishing the water needed, then the well would have to be checked to see why it did not. The parents of the children going to school would know the one to tell to check this out. Mr. Wood! He was the one that had the tools needed and he lived nearby. He had a Divining rod that could be used to tell where a spring of water

was located to dig a well. He also could tell if this stream had dried up or needed to be dug deeper. The younger men were willing to follow his directions and would be ready to volunteer, to go down in the well to clean out any mud or debris, and to dig deeper if this was needed. To get down in the well was a chore. Several men would hold ropes that were looped around the person to be let down, along with the tools needed to dig. Then they would have to lift these from the bottom of the well. The man going down to the bottom would hold to the ropes and stretch his legs from the sides and bounce down easily. He would then call out what he found. The tools would then be lowered to him, as he asked for them. Tools needed could be a shovel, pick ax, large bucket or any other tool anyone might suggest. He would fill the bucket and pull the rope the bucket was attached to, and the men would pull the bucket up and empty it and lower it again and again to him.

This could take all day. When the well was cleaned out and water began to flow again, it would be several days before anyone would be able to drink this water.

At the end of the school year was a celebration time commencement program, which was a school play. I got the part of the angel, and Mama made my outfit out of white crepe paper. I felt so special! All the children had parts to play. Our folks came to see the play and clapped their hand for us. We all felt special!

The little schools like ours were later consolidated with another larger school near us. A big yellow school bus came by our house to pick us up to take us to this school. The bus had benches to sit on. There were two long benches in the center of the bus and one long bench on either side of the bus. It was the first time many of us had ever ridden on a bus. We were afraid that we would never get back home and see our folks again. Some of us cried, as a man we did not know drove the bus. He had a handle he used to open and close the bus door, to let us in or out of the bus.

The new school was a brick building and had a long hall in the center of it with classrooms on either side of the hall. Mid-way in the hall were the indoor toilets. Many of us had never used indoor toilets before. The first time I went to the new type of toilet, I came out of a door in the hallway and did not know which way to go and I went the wrong way. I was at the older children's end of the hall, and they laughed at me, and I wet my clothes (because I was so afraid.)

There were more teachers, and even male teachers, at this school, and more students and better desks. We still took our lunches, and some even had lunch boxes to take their lunches to school in. My lunch was wrapped in brown paper and it was put in a small paper bag. There was a recess in the morning and one in the afternoon and at lunch we had a time to play.

We only had two holidays, Thanksgiving and Christmas. When special people came to visit the school, we all were told to go to the auditorium, which was a large room with many seats that had arm rests on them. The floor was not level. It slanted down toward the front where the stage was, and the speakers sat in chairs until their time to speak came.

Plays were held here and many people came to see and hear those that had parts in the plays recite and act.

As we grew older and learned more, we were promoted to another grade at the end of the school year. We got our report cards at the end of the month to take home for our folks to see and sign their name, making sure they had seen them. There was a big celebration, at the end of the school year. This was called, "Graduation." Those that finished the eleventh grade wore a cap and a gown. The boys wore blue and the girls wore white gowns and they all had funny flat caps with a tassel on one side. When they got their diploma, the tassel was put on the other side of the cap. Graduates sat on the stage with their teachers.

There were never many students to graduate. Some students quit school early for many reasons. Some had to help work on the farm, some got married and some moved away from the area. I quit school in August, before school started in September.

Mama had bought me a new Sunday dress, when she got the material to make my school clothes (when Daddy sold peanuts,) and I had never worn it.

That Saturday, I had a date, and we were late getting in from our Saturday visit to town. Mama, said, "Hurry and do your night chores, now before its time for your fellow to get here." It was the first time I ever remember talking back to Mama. I said, "If the cows never get milked today, I am not milking them!" She did not say a word, just looked at me! That "look" said too much! She got the bucket and did the milking. I hurried and got dressed, in my new dress and hoped "he" would get here before she finished milking the cows. He did!

A minister married us at his home. We came back to my house. My sister and her husband were there and they were all— Daddy, my baby brother, my sister and her husband —sitting in the front room and Mama was leaned back in her straight chair near the fireplace. She gave me that 'look' and said, "What have you gone and done?! Here I started a new life! As a "married woman!"

I packed a few clothes to take with me to his parent's house. We lived with them from then on for several years. They were farmers too, but they did not farm as my parents did. It was like I was in a different country! At this time, his mother milked the cow and did the cooking on a different kind of stove than the one my Mama used. No Chores to do!? No one required anything of me to do!

My family had recently gotten electricity and we had electric lights. Here at his house, they had electricity from a battery operation they had made. I was so impressed! I could only imagine anyone being that smart!

Now, I was company for a while!

Farming in 1930 & 1940's

Order by Mail: $30.00
303 E. Price Street
Sylvester, GA 31791
229-776-4258

SARAH SENKBEIL

*No Electricity
*Mule Power
*Survival

*Neighbors swapped
items needed

*Make do with
what we had!

"Company's Coming"